Further Praise for *The Volatility Surface*

"As an experienced practitioner, Jim Gatheral succeeds admirably in combining an accessible exposition of the foundations of stochastic volatility modeling with valuable guidance on the calibration and implementation of leading volatility models in practice."
—Eckhard Platen, Chair in Quantitative Finance, University of Technology, Sydney

"Dr. Jim Gatheral is one of Wall Street's very best regarding the practical use and understanding of volatility modeling. *The Volatility Surface* reflects his in-depth knowledge about local volatility, stochastic volatility, jumps, the dynamic of the volatility surface and how it affects standard options, exotic options, variance and volatility swaps, and much more. If you are interested in volatility and derivatives, you need this book!"
—Espen Gaarder Haug, option trader, and author to *The Complete Guide to Option Pricing Formulas*

"Anybody who is interested in going beyond Black-Scholes should read this book. And anybody who is not interested in going beyond Black-Scholes isn't going far!"
—Mark Davis, Professor of Mathematics, Imperial College London

"This book provides a comprehensive treatment of subjects essential for anyone working in the field of option pricing. Many technical topics are presented in an elegant and intuitively clear way. It will be indispensable not only at trading desks but also for teaching courses on modern derivatives and will definitely serve as a source of inspiration for new research."
—Anna Shepeleva, Vice President, ING Group

Founded in 1807, John Wiley & Sons is the oldest independent publishing company in the United States. With offices in North America, Europe, Australia, and Asia, Wiley is globally committed to developing and marketing print and electronic products and services for our customers' professional and personal knowledge and understanding.

The Wiley Finance series contains books written specifically for finance and investment professionals as well as sophisticated individual investors and their financial advisors. Book topics range from portfolio management to e-commerce, risk management, financial engineering, valuation, and financial instrument analysis, as well as much more.

For a list of available titles, please visit our Web site at www.WileyFinance.com.

The Volatility Surface

A Practitioner's Guide

JIM GATHERAL

Foreword by Nassim Nicholas Taleb

WILEY

John Wiley & Sons, Inc.

Published by John Wiley & Sons, Inc., Hoboken, New Jersey.
Published simultaneously in Canada.

For general information on our other products and services or for technical support, please
contact our Customer Care Department within the United States at (800) 762-2974, outside
the United States at (317) 572-3993 or fax (317) 572-4002.

Wiley also publishes its books in a variety of electronic formats. Some content that appears in
print may not be available in electronic formats. For more information about Wiley products,
visit our Web site at www.wiley.com.

ISBN-13 978-0-471-79251-2
ISBN-10 0-471-79251-9

Library of Congress Cataloging-in-Publication Data:

Gatheral, Jim, 1957–
   The volatility surface : a practitioner's guide / by Jim Gatheral ; foreword
by Nassim Nicholas Taleb.
        p. cm.—(Wiley finance series)
   Includes index.
   ISBN-13: 978-0-471-79251-2 (cloth)
   ISBN-10: 0-471-79251-9 (cloth)
   1. Options (Finance)—Prices—Mathematical models. 2.
Stocks—Prices—Mathematical models. I. Title. II. Series.
   HG6024. A3G38 2006
   332.63'2220151922—dc22

                                                                      200600997

Printed in the United States of America.

10 9 8 7 6 5 4

To Yukiko and Ayako

Contents

Figures

Tables

Foreword

I

Jim has given round six of these lectures on volatility modeling at the Courant Institute of New York University, slowly purifying these notes. I witnessed and became addicted to their slow maturation from the first time he jotted down these equations during the winter of 2000, to the most recent one in the spring of 2006. It was similar to the progressive distillation of good alcohol: exactly seven times; at every new stage you can see the text gaining in crispness, clarity, and concision. Like Jim's lectures, these chapters are to the point, with maximal simplicity though never less than warranted by the topic, devoid of fluff and side distractions, delivering the exact subject without any attempt to boast his (extraordinary) technical skills.

The class became popular. By the second year we got yelled at by the university staff because too many nonpaying practitioners showed up to the lecture, depriving the (paying) students of seats. By the third or fourth year, the material of this book became a quite standard text, with Jim G.'s lecture notes circulating among instructors. His treatment of local volatility and stochastic models became the standard.

As colecturers, Jim G. and I agreed to attend each other's sessions, but as more than just spectators—turning out to be colecturers in the literal sense, that is, synchronously. He and I heckled each other, making sure that not a single point went undisputed, to the point of other members of the faculty coming to attend this strange class with disputatious instructors trying to tear apart each other's statements, looking for the smallest hole in the arguments. Nor were the arguments always dispassionate: students soon got to learn from Jim my habit of ordering white wine with read meat; in return, I pointed out clear deficiencies in his French, which he pronounces with a sometimes incomprehensible Scottish accent. I realized the value of the course when I started lecturing at other universities. The contrast was such that I had to return very quickly.

II

The difference between Jim Gatheral and other members of the quant community lies in the following: To many, models provide a representation of asset price dynamics, under some constraints. Business school finance professors have a tendency to believe (for some reason) that these provide a top-down statistical mapping of reality. This interpretation is also shared by many of those who have not been exposed to activity of risk-taking, or the constraints of empirical reality.

But not to Jim G. who has both traded and led a career as a quant. To him, these stochastic volatility models cannot make such claims, or should not make such claims. They are not to be deemed a top-down dogmatic representation of reality, rather a tool to insure that all instruments are consistently priced with respect to each other–that is, to satisfy the golden rule of absence of arbitrage. *An operator should not be capable of deriving a profit in replicating a financial instrument by using a combination of other ones.* A model should do the job of insuring maximal consistency between, say, a European digital option of a given maturity, and a call price of another one. The best model is the one that satisfies such constraints while making minimal claims about the true probability distribution of the world.

I recently discovered the strength of his thinking as follows. When, by the fifth or so lecture series I realized that the world needed Mandelbrot-style power-law or scalable distributions, I found that the models he proposed of fudging the volatility surface was compatible with these models. How? You just need to raise volatilities of out-of-the-money options in a specific way, and the volatility surface becomes consistent with the scalable power laws.

Jim Gatheral is a natural and intuitive mathematician; attending his lecture you can watch this effortless virtuosity that the Italians call *sprezzatura*. I see more of it in this book, as his awful handwriting on the blackboard is greatly enhanced by the aesthetics of LaTeX.

—Nassim Nicholas Taleb[1]

June, 2006

---

[1] Author, *Dynamic Hedging* and *Fooled by Randomness*.

Preface

E ver since the advent of the Black-Scholes option pricing formula, the study of implied volatility has become a central preoccupation for both academics and practitioners. As is well known, actual option prices rarely if ever conform to the predictions of the formula because the idealized assumptions required for it to hold don't apply in the real world. Consequently, implied volatility (the volatility input to the Black-Scholes formula that generates the market price) in general depends on the strike and the expiration of the option. The collection of all such implied volatilities is known as the volatility surface.

This book concerns itself with understanding the volatility surface; that is, why options are priced as they are and what it is that analysis of stock returns can tell us about how options ought to be priced.

Pricing is consistently emphasized over hedging, although hedging and replication arguments are often used to generate results. Partly, that's because pricing is key: How a claim is hedged affects only the width of the resulting distribution of returns and not the expectation. On average, no amount of clever hedging can make up for an initial mispricing. Partly, it's because hedging in practice can be complicated and even more of an art than pricing.

Throughout the book, the importance of examining different dynamical assumptions is stressed as is the importance of building intuition in general. The aim of the book is not to just present results but rather to provide the reader with ways of thinking about and solving practical problems that should have many other areas of application. By the end of the book, the reader should have gained substantial intuition for the latest theory underlying options pricing as well as some feel for the history and practice of trading in the equity derivatives markets. With luck, the reader will also be infected with some of the excitement that continues to surround the trading, marketing, pricing, hedging, and risk management of derivatives.

As its title implies, this book is written by a practitioner for practitioners. Amongst other things, it contains a detailed derivation of the Heston model and explanations of many other popular models such as SVJ, SVJJ, SABR, and CreditGrades. The reader will also find explanations of the characteristics of various types of exotic options from the humble barrier option to the super exotic Napoleon. One of the themes of this book is the representation of implied volatility in terms of a weighted average over all possible future volatility scenarios. This representation is not only explained but is applied to help understand the impact of different modeling assumptions on the shape and dynamics of volatility surfaces—a topic of fundamental interest to traders as well as quants. Along the way, various practical results and tricks are presented and explained. Finally, the hot topic of volatility derivatives is exhaustively covered with detailed presentations of the latest research.

Academics may also find the book useful not just as a guide to the current state of research in volatility modeling but also to provide practical context for their work. Practitioners have one huge advantage over academics: They never have to worry about whether or not their work will be interesting to others. This book can thus be viewed as one practitioner's guide to what is interesting and useful.

In short, my hope is that the book will prove useful to anyone interested in the volatility surface whether academic or practitioner.

Readers familiar with my New York University Courant Institute lecture notes will surely recognize the contents of this book. I hope that even aficionados of the lecture notes will find something of extra value in the book. The material has been expanded; there are more and better figures; and there's now an index.

The lecture notes on which this book is based were originally targeted at graduate students in the final semester of a three-semester Master's Program in Financial Mathematics. Students entering the program have undergraduate degrees in quantitative subjects such as mathematics, physics, or engineering. Some are part-time students already working in the industry looking to deepen their understanding of the mathematical aspects of their jobs, others are looking to obtain the necessary mathematical and financial background for a career in the financial industry. By the time they reach the third semester, students have studied financial mathematics, computing and basic probability and stochastic processes.

It follows that to get the most out of this book, the reader should have a level of familiarity with options theory and financial markets that could be obtained from Wilmott (2000), for example. To be able to follow the mathematics, basic knowledge of probability and stochastic calculus such as could be obtained by reading Neftci (2000) or Mikosch (1999) are required. Nevertheless, my hope is that a reader willing to take the mathematical results on trust will still be able to follow the explanations.

HOW THIS BOOK IS ORGANIZED

The first half of the book from Chapters 1 to 5 focuses on setting up the theoretical framework. The latter chapters of the book are more oriented towards practical applications. The split is not rigorous, however, and there are practical applications in the first few chapters and theoretical constructions in the last chapter, reflecting that life, at least the life of a practicing quant, is not split into neat boxes.

Chapter 1 provides an explanation of stochastic and local volatility; local variance is shown to be the risk-neutral expectation of instantaneous variance, a result that is applied repeatedly in later chapters. In Chapter 2, we present the still supremely popular Heston model and derive the Heston European option pricing formula. We also show how to simulate the Heston model.

In Chapter 3, we derive a powerful representation for implied volatility in terms of local volatility. We apply this to build intuition and derive some properties of the implied volatility surface generated by the Heston model and compare with the empirically observed SPX surface. We deduce that stochastic volatility cannot be the whole story.

In Chapter 4, we choose specific numerical values for the parameters of the Heston model, specifically $\rho = -1$ as originally studied by Heston and Nandi. We demonstrate that an approximate formula for implied volatility derived in Chapter 3 works particularly well in this limit. As a result, we are able to find parameters of local volatility and stochastic volatility models that generate almost identical European option prices. We use these parameters repeatedly in subsequent chapters to illustrate the model-dependence of various claims.

In Chapter 5, we explore the modeling of jumps. First we show why jumps are required. We then introduce characteristic function techniques and apply these to the computation of implied volatilities in models with jumps. We conclude by showing that the SVJ model (stochastic volatility with jumps in the stock price) is capable of generating a volatility surface that has most of the features of the empirical surface. Throughout, we build intuition as to how jumps should affect the shape of the volatility surface.

In Chapter 6, we apply our work on jumps to Merton's jump-to-ruin model of default. We also explain the CreditGrades model. In passing, we touch on capital structure arbitrage and offer the first glimpse into the less than ideal world of real trading, explaining how large losses were incurred by market makers.

In Chapter 7, we examine the asymptotic properties of the volatility surface showing that all models with stochastic volatility and jumps generate volatility surfaces that are roughly the same shape. In Chapter 8, we show

how the dynamics of volatility can be deduced from the time series properties of volatility surfaces. We also show why it is that the dynamics of the volatility surfaces generated by local volatility models are highly unrealistic.

In Chapter 9, we present various types of barrier option and show how intuition may be developed for these by studying two simple limiting cases. We test our intuition (successfully) by applying it to the relative valuation of barrier options under stochastic and local volatility. The reflection principle and the concepts of quasi-static hedging and put-call symmetry are presented and applied.

In Chapter 10, we study in detail three actual exotic cliquet transactions that happen to have matured so that we can explore both pricing and ex post performance. Specifically, we study a locally capped and globally floored cliquet, a reverse cliquet, and a Napoleon. Followers of the financial press no doubt already recognize these deal types as having been the cause of substantial pain to some dealers.

Finally, in Chapter 11, the longest of all, we focus on the pricing and hedging of claims whose underlying is quadratic variation. In so doing, we will present some of the most elegant and robust results in financial mathematics, thereby explaining in part why the market in volatility derivatives is surprisingly active and liquid.

—Jim Gatheral

Acknowledgments

I am grateful to more people than I could possibly list here for their help, support and encouragement over the years. First of all, I owe a debt of gratitude to my present and former colleagues, in particular to my Merrill Lynch quant colleagues Jining Han, Chiyan Luo and Yonathan Epelbaum. Second, like all practitioners, my education is partly thanks to those academics and practitioners who openly published their work. Since the bibliography is not meant to be a complete list of references but rather just a list of sources for the present text, there are many people who have made great contributions to the field and strongly influenced my work that are not explicitly mentioned or referenced. To these people, please be sure I am grateful to all of you.

There are a few people who had a much more direct hand in this project to whom explicit thanks are due here: to Nassim Taleb, my co-lecturer at Courant who through good-natured heckling helped shape the contents of my lectures, to Peter Carr, Bruno Dupire and Marco Avellaneda for helpful and insightful conversations and finally to Neil Chriss for sharing some good writing tips and for inviting me to lecture at Courant in the first place. I am absolutely indebted to Peter Friz, my one-time teaching assistant at NYU and now lecturer at the Statistical Laboratory in Cambridge; Peter painstakingly read my lectures notes, correcting them often and suggesting improvements. Without him, there is no doubt that there would have been no book. My thanks are also due to him and to Bruno Dupire for reading a late draft of the manuscript and making useful suggestions. I also wish to thank my editors at Wiley: Pamela Van Giessen, Jennifer MacDonald and Todd Tedesco for their help. Remaining errors are of course mine.

Sincere thanks to Jining Han, James LaDue, Roger Lord, Craig Nelson, Jan Obłój and Fahmi Zaidi for their eagle eyes and close read of earlier printings. The typos they noted are corrected in this printing.

Last but by no means least, I am deeply grateful to Yukiko and Ayako for putting up with me.

Stochastic Volatility
and Local Volatility

In this chapter, we begin our exploration of the volatility surface by introducing stochastic volatility—the notion that volatility varies in a random fashion. Local variance is then shown to be a conditional expectation of the instantaneous variance so that various quantities of interest (such as option prices) may sometimes be computed as though future volatility were deterministic rather than stochastic.

STOCHASTIC VOLATILITY

That it might make sense to model volatility as a random variable should be clear to the most casual observer of equity markets. To be convinced, one need only recall the stock market crash of October 1987. Nevertheless, given the success of the Black-Scholes model in parsimoniously describing market options prices, it's not immediately obvious what the benefits of making such a modeling choice might be.

Stochastic volatility (SV) models are useful because they explain in a self-consistent way why options with different strikes and expirations have different Black-Scholes implied volatilities—that is, the "volatility smile." Moreover, unlike alternative models that can fit the smile (such as local volatility models, for example), SV models assume realistic dynamics for the underlying. Although SV price processes are sometimes accused of being *ad hoc*, on the contrary, they can be viewed as arising from Brownian motion subordinated to a random clock. This clock time, often referred to as *trading time*, may be identified with the volume of trades or the frequency of trading (Clark 1973); the idea is that as trading activity fluctuates, so does volatility.

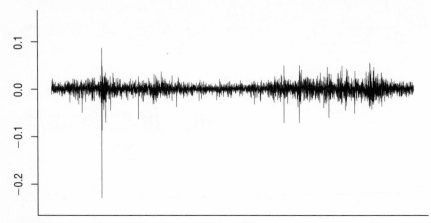

FIGURE 1.1 SPX daily log returns from December 31, 1984, to December 31, 2004. Note the −22.9% return on October 19, 1987!

From a hedging perspective, traders who use the Black-Scholes model must continuously change the volatility assumption in order to match market prices. Their hedge ratios change accordingly in an uncontrolled way: SV models bring some order into this chaos.

A practical point that is more pertinent to a recurring theme of this book is that the prices of exotic options given by models based on Black-Scholes assumptions can be wildly wrong and dealers in such options are motivated to find models that can take the volatility smile into account when pricing these.

In Figure 1.1, we plot the log returns of SPX over a 15-year period; we see that large moves follow large moves and small moves follow small moves (so-called "volatility clustering"). In Figure 1.2, we plot the frequency distribution of SPX log returns over the 77-year period from 1928 to 2005. We see that this distribution is highly peaked and fat-tailed relative to the normal distribution. The Q-Q plot in Figure 1.3 shows just how extreme the tails of the empirical distribution of returns are relative to the normal distribution. (This plot would be a straight line if the empirical distribution were normal.)

Fat tails and the high central peak are characteristics of mixtures of distributions with different variances. This motivates us to model variance as a random variable. The volatility clustering feature implies that volatility (or variance) is auto-correlated. In the model, this is a consequence of the mean reversion of volatility.*

---

*Note that simple jump-diffusion models do not have this property. After a jump, the stock price volatility does not change.

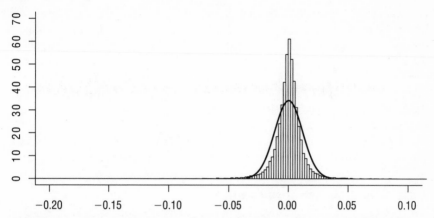

FIGURE 1.2 Frequency distribution of (77 years of) SPX daily log returns compared with the normal distribution. Although the −22.9% return on October 19, 1987, is not directly visible, the x-axis has been extended to the left to accommodate it!

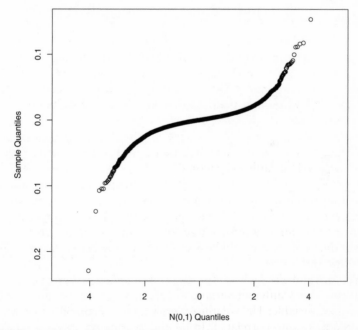

FIGURE 1.3 Q-Q plot of SPX daily log returns compared with the normal distribution. Note the extreme tails.

There is a simple economic argument that justifies the mean reversion of volatility. (The same argument is used to justify the mean reversion of interest rates.) Consider the distribution of the volatility of IBM in 100 years time. If volatility were not mean reverting (i.e., if the distribution of volatility were not stable), the probability of the volatility of IBM being between 1% and 100% would be rather low. Since we believe that it is overwhelmingly likely that the volatility of IBM would in fact lie in that range, we deduce that volatility must be mean reverting.

Having motivated the description of variance as a mean reverting random variable, we are now ready to derive the valuation equation.

Derivation of the Valuation Equation

In this section, we follow Wilmott (2000) closely. Suppose that the stock price S and its variance v satisfy the following SDEs:

$$dS_t = \mu_t S_t \, dt + \sqrt{v_t} \, S_t \, dZ_1 \tag{1.1}$$

$$dv_t = \alpha(S_t, v_t, t) \, dt + \eta \, \beta(S_t, v_t, t) \, \sqrt{v_t} dZ_2 \tag{1.2}$$

with

$$\langle dZ_1 \, dZ_2 \rangle = \rho \, dt$$

where μ_t is the (deterministic) instantaneous drift of stock price returns, η is the volatility of volatility and ρ is the correlation between random stock price returns and changes in v_t. dZ_1 and dZ_2 are Wiener processes.

The stochastic process (1.1) followed by the stock price is equivalent to the one assumed in the derivation of Black and Scholes (1973). This ensures that the standard time-dependent volatility version of the Black-Scholes formula (as derived in Section 8.6 of Wilmott (2000) for example) may be retrieved in the limit $\eta \to 0$. In practical applications, this is a key requirement of a stochastic volatility option pricing model as practitioners' intuition for the behavior of option prices is invariably expressed within the framework of the Black-Scholes formula.

In contrast, the stochastic process (1.2) followed by the variance is very general. We don't assume anything about the functional forms of $\alpha(\cdot)$ and $\beta(\cdot)$. In particular, we don't assume a square root process for variance.

In the Black-Scholes case, there is only one source of randomness, the stock price, which can be hedged with stock. In the present case, random changes in volatility also need to be hedged in order to form a riskless portfolio. So we set up a portfolio Π containing the option being priced, whose value we denote by $V(S, v, t)$, a quantity $-\Delta$ of the stock and a quantity $-\Delta_1$ of another asset whose value V_1 depends on volatility. We have

$$\Pi = V - \Delta S - \Delta_1 V_1$$

The change in this portfolio in a time dt is given by

$$
\begin{aligned}
d\Pi = {} & \left\{ \frac{\partial V}{\partial t} + \frac{1}{2} v S^2 \frac{\partial^2 V}{\partial S^2} + \rho \eta v \beta S \frac{\partial^2 V}{\partial v \, \partial S} + \frac{1}{2} \eta^2 v \beta^2 \frac{\partial^2 V}{\partial v^2} \right\} dt \\
& - \Delta_1 \left\{ \frac{\partial V_1}{\partial t} + \frac{1}{2} v S^2 \frac{\partial^2 V_1}{\partial S^2} + \rho \eta v \beta S \frac{\partial^2 V_1}{\partial v \, \partial S} + \frac{1}{2} \eta^2 v \beta^2 \frac{\partial^2 V_1}{\partial v^2} \right\} dt \\
& + \left\{ \frac{\partial V}{\partial S} - \Delta_1 \frac{\partial V_1}{\partial S} - \Delta \right\} dS \\
& + \left\{ \frac{\partial V}{\partial v} - \Delta_1 \frac{\partial V_1}{\partial v} \right\} dv
\end{aligned}
$$

where, for clarity, we have eliminated the explicit dependence on t of the state variables S_t and v_t and the dependence of α and β on the state variables. To make the portfolio instantaneously risk-free, we must choose

$$\frac{\partial V}{\partial S} - \Delta_1 \frac{\partial V_1}{\partial S} - \Delta = 0$$

to eliminate dS terms, and

$$\frac{\partial V}{\partial v} - \Delta_1 \frac{\partial V_1}{\partial v} = 0$$

to eliminate dv terms. This leaves us with

$$
\begin{aligned}
d\Pi = {} & \left\{ \frac{\partial V}{\partial t} + \frac{1}{2} v S^2 \frac{\partial^2 V}{\partial S^2} + \rho \eta v \beta S \frac{\partial^2 V}{\partial v \partial S} + \frac{1}{2} \eta^2 v \beta^2 \frac{\partial^2 V}{\partial v^2} \right\} dt \\
& - \Delta_1 \left\{ \frac{\partial V_1}{\partial t} + \frac{1}{2} v S^2 \frac{\partial^2 V_1}{\partial S^2} + \rho \eta v \beta S \frac{\partial^2 V_1}{\partial v \partial S} + \frac{1}{2} \eta^2 v \beta^2 \frac{\partial^2 V_1}{\partial v^2} \right\} dt \\
& = r \Pi \, dt \\
& = r(V - \Delta S - \Delta_1 V_1) \, dt
\end{aligned}
$$

where we have used the fact that the return on a risk-free portfolio must equal the risk-free rate r, which we will assume to be deterministic for our purposes. Collecting all V terms on the left-hand side and all V_1 terms on the right-hand side, we get

$$
\frac{\frac{\partial V}{\partial t} + \frac{1}{2}vS^2\frac{\partial^2 V}{\partial S^2} + \rho\eta v\beta S\frac{\partial^2 V}{\partial v\partial S} + \frac{1}{2}\eta^2 v\beta^2\frac{\partial^2 V}{\partial v^2} + rS\frac{\partial V}{\partial S} - rV}{\frac{\partial V}{\partial v}}
$$

$$
= \frac{\frac{\partial V_1}{\partial t} + \frac{1}{2}vS^2\frac{\partial^2 V_1}{\partial S^2} + \rho\eta v\beta S\frac{\partial^2 V_1}{\partial v\partial S} + \frac{1}{2}\eta^2 v\beta^2\frac{\partial^2 V_1}{\partial v^2} + rS\frac{\partial V_1}{\partial S} - rV_1}{\frac{\partial V_1}{\partial v}}
$$

The left-hand side is a function of V only and the right-hand side is a function of V_1 only. The only way that this can be is for both sides to be equal to some function f of the *independent* variables S, v and t. We deduce that

$$
\frac{\partial V}{\partial t} + \frac{1}{2}vS^2\frac{\partial^2 V}{\partial S^2} + \rho\eta v\beta S\frac{\partial^2 V}{\partial v\,\partial S} + \frac{1}{2}\eta^2 v\beta^2\frac{\partial^2 V}{\partial v^2} + rS\frac{\partial V}{\partial S} - rV
$$

$$
= -\left(\alpha - \phi\beta\sqrt{v}\right)\frac{\partial V}{\partial v} \tag{1.3}
$$

where, without loss of generality, we have written the arbitrary function f of S, v and t as $\left(\alpha - \phi\beta\sqrt{v}\right)$, where α and β are the drift and volatility functions from the SDE (1.2) for instantaneous variance.

The Market Price of Volatility Risk $\phi(S, v, t)$ is called the market price of volatility risk. To see why, we again follow Wilmott's argument.

Consider the portfolio Π_1 consisting of a delta-hedged (but not vega-hedged) option V. Then

$$
\Pi_1 = V - \frac{\partial V}{\partial S}S
$$

and again applying Itô's lemma,

$$
d\Pi_1 = \left\{\frac{\partial V}{\partial t} + \frac{1}{2}vS^2\frac{\partial^2 V}{\partial S^2} + \rho\eta v\beta S\frac{\partial^2 V}{\partial v\,\partial S} + \frac{1}{2}\eta^2 v\beta^2\frac{\partial^2 V}{\partial v^2}\right\}dt
$$

$$
+ \left\{\frac{\partial V}{\partial S} - \Delta\right\}dS + \left\{\frac{\partial V}{\partial v}\right\}dv
$$

Because the option is delta-hedged, the coefficient of dS is zero and we are left with

$$d\Pi_1 - r\,\Pi_1\,dt$$

$$= \left\{ \frac{\partial V}{\partial t} + \frac{1}{2}vS^2\frac{\partial^2 V}{\partial S^2} + \rho\eta v\beta S\frac{\partial^2 V}{\partial v\partial S} + \frac{1}{2}\eta^2 v\beta^2\frac{\partial^2 V}{\partial v^2} + rS\frac{\partial V}{\partial S} - r\,V \right\}dt$$

$$+ \frac{\partial V}{\partial v}\,dv$$

$$= \beta\sqrt{v}\,\frac{\partial V}{\partial v}\,\left\{\phi(S,v,t)\,dt + \eta\,dZ_2\right\}$$

where we have used both the valuation equation (1.3) and the SDE (1.2) for v. We see that the extra return per unit of volatility risk dZ_2 is given by $\phi(S,v,t)\,dt$ and so in analogy with the Capital Asset Pricing Model, ϕ is known as the *market price of volatility risk*.

Now, defining the *risk-neutral drift* as

$$\alpha' = \alpha - \beta\sqrt{v}\,\phi$$

we see that, as far as pricing of options is concerned, we could have started with the risk-neutral SDE for v,

$$dv = \alpha'\,dt + \beta\sqrt{v}\,dZ_2$$

and got identical results with no explicit price of risk term because we are in the risk-neutral world.

In what follows, we always assume that the SDEs for S and v are in risk-neutral terms because we are invariably interested in fitting models to option prices. Effectively, we assume that we are imputing the risk-neutral measure directly by fitting the parameters of the process that we are imposing.

Were we interested in the connection between the pricing of options and the behavior of the time series of historical returns of the underlying, we would need to understand the connection between the statistical measure under which the drift of the variance process v is α and the risk-neutral process under which the drift of the variance process is α'. From now on, we act as if we are risk-neutral and drop the prime.

LOCAL VOLATILITY

History

Given the computational complexity of stochastic volatility models and the difficulty of fitting parameters to the current prices of vanilla options, practitioners sought a simpler way of pricing exotic options consistently with the volatility skew. Since before Breeden and Litzenberger (1978), it was understood (at least by floor traders) that the risk-neutral density could be derived from the market prices of European options. The breakthrough came when Dupire (1994) and Derman and Kani (1994)* noted that under risk neutrality, there was a unique diffusion process consistent with these distributions. The corresponding unique state-dependent diffusion coefficient $\sigma_L(S, t)$, consistent with current European option prices, is known as the *local volatility function*.

It is unlikely that Dupire, Derman, and Kani ever thought of local volatility as representing a model of how volatilities actually evolve. Rather, it is likely that they thought of local volatilities as representing some kind of average over all possible instantaneous volatilities in a stochastic volatility world (an "effective theory"). Local volatility models do not therefore really represent a separate class of models; the idea is more to make a simplifying assumption that allows practitioners to price exotic options consistently with the known prices of vanilla options.

As if any proof were needed, Dumas, Fleming, and Whaley (1998) performed an empirical analysis that confirmed that the dynamics of the implied volatility surface were not consistent with the assumption of constant local volatilities.

Later on, we show that local volatility is indeed an average over instantaneous volatilities, formalizing the intuition of those practitioners who first introduced the concept.

A Brief Review of Dupire's Work

For a given expiration T and current stock price S_0, the collection $\{C(S_0, K, T)\}$ of undiscounted option prices of different strikes yields the risk-neutral density function φ of the final spot S_T through the relationship

$$C(S_0, K, T) = \int_K^\infty dS_T \, \varphi(S_T, T; S_0)(S_T - K)$$

Differentiate this twice with respect to K to obtain

$$\varphi(K, T; S_0) = \frac{\partial^2 C}{\partial K^2}$$

---

*Dupire published the continuous time theory and Derman and Kani, a discrete time binomial tree version.

so the Arrow-Debreu prices for each expiration may be recovered by twice differentiating the undiscounted option price with respect to K. This process is familiar to any option trader as the construction of an (infinite size) infinitesimally tight butterfly around the strike whose maximum payoff is one.

Given the distribution of final spot prices S_T for each time T conditional on some starting spot price S_0, Dupire shows that there is a unique risk neutral diffusion process which generates these distributions. That is, given the set of all European option prices, we may determine the functional form of the diffusion parameter (local volatility) of the unique risk neutral diffusion process which generates these prices. Noting that the local volatility will in general be a function of the current stock price S_0, we write this process as

$$\frac{dS}{S} = \mu_t \, dt + \sigma \, (S_t, t; S_0) \, dZ$$

Application of Itô's lemma together with risk neutrality, gives rise to a partial differential equation for functions of the stock price, which is a straightforward generalization of Black-Scholes. In particular, the pseudo-probability densities $\varphi \, (K, T; S_0) = \frac{\partial^2 C}{\partial K^2}$ must satisfy the Fokker-Planck equation. This leads to the following equation for the undiscounted option price C in terms of the strike price K:

$$\frac{\partial C}{\partial T} = \frac{\sigma^2 K^2}{2} \frac{\partial^2 C}{\partial K^2} + (r_t - D_t) \left(C - K \frac{\partial C}{\partial K} \right) \tag{1.4}$$

where r_t is the risk-free rate, D_t is the dividend yield and C is short for $C \, (S_0, K, T)$.

Derivation of the Dupire Equation

Suppose the stock price diffuses with risk-neutral drift $\mu_t \, (= r_t - D_t)$ and local volatility $\sigma \, (S, t)$ according to the equation:

$$\frac{dS}{S} = \mu_t \, dt + \sigma \, (S_t, t) \, dZ$$

The undiscounted risk-neutral value $C \, (S_0, K, T)$ of a European option with strike K and expiration T is given by

$$C \, (S_0, K, T) = \int_K^\infty dS_T \, \varphi \, (S_T, T; S_0) \, (S_T - K) \tag{1.5}$$

Here $\varphi\,(S_T, T; S_0)$ is the pseudo-probability density of the final spot at time T. It evolves according to the Fokker-Planck equation:

$$\frac{1}{2}\frac{\partial^2}{\partial S_T^2}\left(\sigma^2 S_T^2\,\varphi\right) - \frac{\partial}{\partial S_T}\left(\mu\,S_T\,\varphi\right) = \frac{\partial\varphi}{\partial T}$$

Differentiating with respect to K gives

$$\frac{\partial C}{\partial K} = -\int_K^\infty dS_T\,\varphi\,(S_T, T; S_0)$$

$$\frac{\partial^2 C}{\partial K^2} = \varphi\,(K, T; S_0)$$

Now, differentiating (1.5) with respect to time gives

$$\frac{\partial C}{\partial T} = \int_K^\infty dS_T\,\left\{\frac{\partial}{\partial T}\varphi\,(S_T, T; S_0)\right\}(S_T - K)$$

$$= \int_K^\infty dS_T\,\left\{\frac{1}{2}\frac{\partial^2}{\partial S_T^2}\left(\sigma^2 S_T^2\varphi\right) - \frac{\partial}{\partial S_T}\left(\mu\,S_T\,\varphi\right)\right\}(S_T - K)$$

Integrating by parts twice gives:

$$\frac{\partial C}{\partial T} = \frac{\sigma^2 K^2}{2}\,\varphi + \int_K^\infty dS_T\,\mu\,S_T\,\varphi$$

$$= \frac{\sigma^2 K^2}{2}\frac{\partial^2 C}{\partial K^2} + \mu\,(T)\left(C - K\frac{\partial C}{\partial K}\right)$$

which is the Dupire equation when the underlying stock has risk-neutral drift μ. That is, the forward price of the stock at time T is given by

$$F_T = S_0\,\exp\left\{\int_0^T dt\,\mu_t\right\}$$

    Were we to express the option price as a function of the forward price $F_T = S_0\,\exp\left\{\int_0^T \mu(t)dt\right\}^*$, we would get the same expression minus the drift term. That is,

$$\frac{\partial C}{\partial T} = \frac{1}{2}\sigma^2 K^2\frac{\partial^2 C}{\partial K^2}$$

---

*From now on, $\mu(T)$ represents the risk-neutral drift of the stock price process, which is the risk-free rate $r(T)$ minus the dividend yield $D(T)$.

where C now represents $C(F_T, K, T)$. Inverting this gives

$$\sigma^2(K, T, S_0) = \frac{\frac{\partial C}{\partial T}}{\frac{1}{2} K^2 \frac{\partial^2 C}{\partial K^2}} \quad (1.6)$$

The right-hand side of equation (1.6) can be computed from known European option prices. So, given a complete set of European option prices for all strikes and expirations, local volatilities are given uniquely by equation (1.6).

We can view equation (1.6) as a *definition* of the local volatility function regardless of what kind of process (stochastic volatility for example) actually governs the evolution of volatility.

Local Volatility in Terms of Implied Volatility

Market prices of options are quoted in terms of Black-Scholes implied volatility $\sigma_{BS}(K, T; S_0)$. In other words, we may write

$$C(S_0, K, T) = C_{BS}(S_0, K, \sigma_{BS}(S_0, K, T), T)$$

It will be more convenient for us to work in terms of two dimensionless variables: the Black-Scholes implied total variance w defined by

$$w(S_0, K, T) := \sigma_{BS}^2(S_0, K, T)\, T$$

and the log-strike y defined by

$$y = \log\left(\frac{K}{F_T}\right)$$

where $F_T = S_0 \exp\left\{\int_0^T dt\, \mu(t)\right\}$ gives the forward price of the stock at time 0. In terms of these variables, the Black-Scholes formula for the future value of the option price becomes

$$C_{BS}(F_T, y, w) = F_T\left\{N(d_1) - e^y N(d_2)\right\}$$

$$= F_T\left\{N\left(-\frac{y}{\sqrt{w}} + \frac{\sqrt{w}}{2}\right) - e^y N\left(-\frac{y}{\sqrt{w}} - \frac{\sqrt{w}}{2}\right)\right\} \quad (1.7)$$

and the Dupire equation (1.4) becomes

$$\frac{\partial C}{\partial T} = \frac{v_L}{2}\left\{\frac{\partial^2 C}{\partial y^2} - \frac{\partial C}{\partial y}\right\} + \mu(T) C \quad (1.8)$$

with $v_L = \sigma^2 (S_0, K, T)$ representing the local variance. Now, by taking derivatives of the Black-Scholes formula, we obtain

$$\frac{\partial^2 C_{BS}}{\partial w^2} = \left(-\frac{1}{8} - \frac{1}{2w} + \frac{y^2}{2w^2}\right) \frac{\partial C_{BS}}{\partial w}$$

$$\frac{\partial^2 C_{BS}}{\partial y \partial w} = \left(\frac{1}{2} - \frac{y}{w}\right) \frac{\partial C_{BS}}{\partial w}$$

$$\frac{\partial^2 C_{BS}}{\partial y^2} - \frac{\partial C_{BS}}{\partial y} = 2 \frac{\partial C_{BS}}{\partial w} \tag{1.9}$$

We may transform equation (1.8) into an equation in terms of implied variance by making the substitutions

$$\frac{\partial C}{\partial y} = \frac{\partial C_{BS}}{\partial y} + \frac{\partial C_{BS}}{\partial w} \frac{\partial w}{\partial y}$$

$$\frac{\partial^2 C}{\partial y^2} = \frac{\partial^2 C_{BS}}{\partial y^2} + 2 \frac{\partial^2 C_{BS}}{\partial y \partial w} \frac{\partial w}{\partial y} + \frac{\partial^2 C_{BS}}{\partial w^2} \left(\frac{\partial w}{\partial y}\right)^2 + \frac{\partial C_{BS}}{\partial w} \frac{\partial^2 w}{\partial y^2}$$

$$\frac{\partial C}{\partial T} = \frac{\partial C_{BS}}{\partial T} + \frac{\partial C_{BS}}{\partial w} \frac{\partial w}{\partial T} = \frac{\partial C_{BS}}{\partial w} \frac{\partial w}{\partial T} + \mu(T) C_{BS}$$

where the last equality follows from the fact that the only explicit dependence of the option price on T in equation (1.7) is through the forward price $F_T = S_0 \exp\left\{\int_0^T dt\, \mu(t)\right\}$. Equation (1.4) now becomes (cancelling $\mu(T) C$ terms on each side)

$$\frac{\partial C_{BS}}{\partial w} \frac{\partial w}{\partial T}$$

$$= \frac{v_L}{2} \left\{ -\frac{\partial C_{BS}}{\partial y} + \frac{\partial^2 C_{BS}}{\partial y^2} - \frac{\partial C_{BS}}{\partial w} \frac{\partial w}{\partial y} + 2 \frac{\partial^2 C_{BS}}{\partial y \partial w} \frac{\partial w}{\partial y} \right.$$

$$\left. + \frac{\partial^2 C_{BS}}{\partial w^2} \left(\frac{\partial w}{\partial y}\right)^2 + \frac{\partial C_{BS}}{\partial w} \frac{\partial^2 w}{\partial y^2} \right\}$$

$$= \frac{v_L}{2} \frac{\partial C_{BS}}{\partial w} \left\{ 2 - \frac{\partial w}{\partial y} + 2 \left(\frac{1}{2} - \frac{y}{w}\right) \frac{\partial w}{\partial y} \right.$$

$$\left. + \left(-\frac{1}{8} - \frac{1}{2w} + \frac{y^2}{2w^2}\right) \left(\frac{\partial w}{\partial y}\right)^2 + \frac{\partial^2 w}{\partial y^2} \right\}$$

Then, taking out a factor of $\frac{\partial C_{BS}}{\partial w}$ and simplifying, we get

$$\frac{\partial w}{\partial T} = v_L \left\{ 1 - \frac{y}{w} \frac{\partial w}{\partial y} + \frac{1}{4} \left(-\frac{1}{4} - \frac{1}{w} + \frac{y^2}{w^2} \right) \left(\frac{\partial w}{\partial y} \right)^2 + \frac{1}{2} \frac{\partial^2 w}{\partial y^2} \right\}$$

Inverting this gives our final result:

$$v_L = \frac{\frac{\partial w}{\partial T}}{1 - \frac{y}{w} \frac{\partial w}{\partial y} + \frac{1}{4} \left(-\frac{1}{4} - \frac{1}{w} + \frac{y^2}{w^2} \right) \left(\frac{\partial w}{\partial y} \right)^2 + \frac{1}{2} \frac{\partial^2 w}{\partial y^2}} \qquad (1.10)$$

Special Case: No Skew*

If the skew $\frac{\partial w}{\partial y}$ is zero, we must have

$$v_L = \frac{\partial w}{\partial T}$$

So the local variance in this case reduces to the forward Black-Scholes implied variance. The solution to this is, of course,

$$w(T) = \int_0^T v_L(t) \, dt$$

Local Variance as a Conditional Expectation of Instantaneous Variance

This result was originally independently derived by Dupire (1996) and Derman and Kani (1998). Following now the elegant derivation by Derman and Kani, assume the same stochastic process for the stock price as in equation (1.1) but write it in terms of the forward price $F_{t,T} = S_t \exp\left\{ \int_t^T ds\, \mu_s \right\}$:

$$dF_{t,T} = \sqrt{v_t} F_{t,T} dZ \qquad (1.11)$$

Note that $dF_{T,T} = dS_T$. The undiscounted value of a European option with strike K expiring at time T is given by

$$C(S_0, K, T) = \mathbb{E}\left[(S_T - K)^+ \right]$$

---

*Note that this implies that $\frac{\partial}{\partial K} \sigma_{BS}(S_0, K, T)$ is zero.

Differentiating once with respect to K gives

$$\frac{\partial C}{\partial K} = -\mathbb{E}\left[\theta\left(S_T - K\right)\right]$$

where $\theta(\cdot)$ is the Heaviside function. Differentiating again with respect to K gives

$$\frac{\partial^2 C}{\partial K^2} = \mathbb{E}\left[\delta\left(S_T - K\right)\right]$$

where $\delta(\cdot)$ is the Dirac δ function.

Now a formal application of Itô's lemma to the terminal payoff of the option (and using $dF_{T,T} = dS_T$) gives the identity

$$d\left(S_T - K\right)^+ = \theta\left(S_T - K\right)dS_T + \frac{1}{2}v_T S_T^2 \delta\left(S_T - K\right)dT$$

Taking conditional expectations of each side, and using the fact that $F_{t,T}$ is a martingale, we get

$$dC = d\mathbb{E}\left[\left(S_T - K\right)^+\right] = \frac{1}{2}\mathbb{E}\left[v_T S_T^2 \delta\left(S_T - K\right)\right]dT$$

Also, we can write

$$\mathbb{E}\left[v_T S_T^2 \delta\left(S_T - K\right)\right] = \mathbb{E}\left[v_T \,|\, S_T = K\right]\frac{1}{2}K^2 \,\mathbb{E}\left[\delta\left(S_T - K\right)\right]$$

$$= \mathbb{E}\left[v_T \,|\, S_T = K\right]\frac{1}{2}K^2 \frac{\partial^2 C}{\partial K^2}$$

Putting this together, we get

$$\frac{\partial C}{\partial T} = \mathbb{E}\left[v_T \,|\, S_T = K\right]\frac{1}{2}K^2 \frac{\partial^2 C}{\partial K^2}$$

Comparing this with the definition of local volatility (equation (1.6)), we see that

$$\sigma^2(K, T, S_0) = \mathbb{E}\left[v_T \,|\, S_T = K\right] \tag{1.12}$$

That is, local variance is the risk-neutral expectation of the instantaneous variance conditional on the final stock price S_T being equal to the strike price K.

CHAPTER 2

The Heston Model

In this chapter, we present the most well-known and popular of all stochastic volatility models, the Heston model, and provide a detailed derivation of the Heston European option valuation formula, implementation of which follows straightforwardly from the derivation. We also show how to discretize the Heston process for Monte Carlo simulation and with some appreciation for the complexity and expense of numerical computations, suggest a main reason for the Heston model's popularity.

THE PROCESS

The Heston model (Heston (1993)) corresponds to choosing $\alpha(S, v_t, t) = -\lambda (v_t - \bar{v})$ and $\beta(S, v, t) = 1$ in equations (1.1) and (1.2). These equations then become

$$dS_t = \mu_t S_t \, dt + \sqrt{v_t} \, S_t \, dZ_1 \tag{2.1}$$

and

$$dv_t = -\lambda (v_t - \bar{v}) \, dt + \eta \sqrt{v_t} \, dZ_2 \tag{2.2}$$

with

$$\langle dZ_1 \, dZ_2 \rangle = \rho \, dt$$

where λ is the speed of reversion of v_t to its long-term mean $\bar{v}$.

The process followed by the instantaneous variance v_t may be recognized as a version of the square root process described by Cox, Ingersoll, and Ross (1985). It is a (jump-free) special case of a so-called *affine jump diffusion (AJD)* that is roughly speaking a jump-diffusion process for which the drifts and covariances and jump intensities are linear in the state vector, which is $\{x, v\}$ in this case with $x = \log(S)$. Duffie, Pan, and Singleton (2000) show that AJD processes are analytically tractable in general. The solution technique involves computing an "extended transform", which in the Heston case is a conventional Fourier transform.

We now substitute the above values for $\alpha(S, v, t)$ and $\beta(S, v, t)$ into the general valuation equation (1.3). We obtain

$$\frac{\partial V}{\partial t} + \frac{1}{2} v S^2 \frac{\partial^2 V}{\partial S^2} + \rho \eta v S \frac{\partial^2 V}{\partial v \partial S} + \frac{1}{2} \eta^2 v \frac{\partial^2 V}{\partial v^2} + r S \frac{\partial V}{\partial S} - r V$$

$$= \lambda(v - \overline{v}) \frac{\partial V}{\partial v} \quad (2.3)$$

In Heston's original paper, the price of risk is assumed to be linear in the instantaneous variance v in order to retain the form of the equation under the transformation from the statistical (or real) measure to the risk-neutral measure. In contrast, as in Chapter 1, we assume that the Heston process, with parameters fitted to option prices, generates the risk-neutral measure so the market price of volatility risk φ in the general valuation equation (1.3) is set to zero in equation (2.3). Since we are only interested in pricing, and we assume that the pricing measure is recoverable from European option prices, we are indifferent to the statistical measure.

THE HESTON SOLUTION FOR EUROPEAN OPTIONS

This section follows the original derivation of the Heston formula for the value of a European-style option in Heston (1993) pretty closely but with some changes in intermediate definitions as explained later on.

Before solving equation (2.3) with the appropriate boundary conditions, we can simplify it by making some suitable changes of variable. Let K be the strike price of the option, T time to expiration, $F_{t,T}$ the time T forward price of the stock index and $x := \log\left(F_{t,T}/K\right)$.

Further, suppose that we consider only the future value to expiration C of the European option price rather than its value today and define $\tau = T - t$. Then equation (2.3) simplifies to

$$-\frac{\partial C}{\partial \tau} + \frac{1}{2} v C_{11} - \frac{1}{2} v C_1 + \frac{1}{2} \eta^2 v C_{22} + \rho \eta v C_{12} - \lambda(v - \overline{v}) C_2 = 0$$

$$(2.4)$$

where the subscripts 1 and 2 refer to differentiation with respect to x and v respectively.

According to Duffie, Pan, and Singleton (2000), the solution of equation (2.4) has the form

$$C(x, v, \tau) = K \left\{ e^x P_1(x, v, \tau) - P_0(x, v, \tau) \right\} \qquad (2.5)$$

where, exactly as in the Black-Scholes formula, the first term in the brackets represents the pseudo-expectation of the final index level given that the option is in-the-money and the second term represents the pseudo-probability of exercise.

Substituting the proposed solution (2.5) into equation (2.4) implies that P_0 and P_1 must satisfy the equation

$$-\frac{\partial P_j}{\partial \tau} + \frac{1}{2} v \frac{\partial^2 P_j}{\partial x^2} - \left(\frac{1}{2} - j \right) v \frac{\partial P_j}{\partial x} + \frac{1}{2} \eta^2 v \frac{\partial^2 P_j}{\partial v^2} + \rho \eta v \frac{\partial^2 P_j}{\partial x \partial v}$$

$$+ (a - b_j v) \frac{\partial P_j}{\partial v} = 0 \qquad (2.6)$$

for $j = 0, 1$ where

$$a = \lambda \bar{v}, \quad b_j = \lambda - j \rho \eta$$

subject to the terminal condition

$$\lim_{\tau \to 0} P_j(x, v, \tau) = \begin{cases} 1 \text{ if } x > 0 \\ 0 \text{ if } x \le 0 \end{cases}$$

$$:= \theta(x) \qquad (2.7)$$

We solve equation (2.6) subject to the condition (2.7) using a Fourier transform technique. To this end define the Fourier transform of P_j through

$$\tilde{P}(u, v, \tau) = \int_{-\infty}^{\infty} dx \, e^{-iux} P(x, v, \tau)$$

Then

$$\tilde{P}(u, v, 0) = \int_{-\infty}^{\infty} dx \, e^{-iux} \theta(x) = \frac{1}{iu}$$

The inverse transform is given by

$$P(x, v, \tau) = \int_{-\infty}^{\infty} \frac{du}{2\pi} e^{iux} \tilde{P}(u, v, \tau) \qquad (2.8)$$

Substituting this into equation (2.6) gives

$$-\frac{\partial \tilde{P}_j}{\partial \tau} - \frac{1}{2} u^2 v \tilde{P}_j - \left(\frac{1}{2} - j\right) i u v \tilde{P}_j$$

$$+ \frac{1}{2} \eta^2 v \frac{\partial^2 \tilde{P}_j}{\partial v^2} + \rho \eta i u v \frac{\partial \tilde{P}_j}{\partial v} + (a - b_j v) \frac{\partial \tilde{P}_j}{\partial v} = 0 \qquad (2.9)$$

Now define

$$\alpha = -\frac{u^2}{2} - \frac{iu}{2} + iju$$

$$\beta = \lambda - \rho \eta j - \rho \eta i u$$

$$\gamma = \frac{\eta^2}{2}$$

Then equation (2.9) becomes

$$v \left\{ \alpha \tilde{P}_j - \beta \frac{\partial \tilde{P}_j}{\partial v} + \gamma \frac{\partial^2 \tilde{P}_j}{\partial v^2} \right\} + a \frac{\partial \tilde{P}_j}{\partial v} - \frac{\partial \tilde{P}_j}{\partial \tau} = 0 \qquad (2.10)$$

Now substitute

$$\tilde{P}_j(u, v, \tau) = \exp \{C(u, \tau) \bar{v} + D(u, \tau) v\} \, \tilde{P}_j(u, v, 0)$$

$$= \frac{1}{iu} \exp \{C(u, \tau) \bar{v} + D(u, \tau) v\}$$

It follows that

$$\frac{\partial \tilde{P}_j}{\partial \tau} = \left\{ \bar{v} \frac{\partial C}{\partial \tau} + v \frac{\partial D}{\partial \tau} \right\} \tilde{P}_j$$

$$\frac{\partial \tilde{P}_j}{\partial v} = D \tilde{P}_j$$

$$\frac{\partial^2 \tilde{P}_j}{\partial v^2} = D^2 \tilde{P}_j$$

Then equation (2.10) is satisfied if

$$\frac{\partial C}{\partial \tau} = \lambda D$$

$$\frac{\partial D}{\partial \tau} = \alpha - \beta D + \gamma D^2$$

$$= \gamma (D - r_+)(D - r_-) \qquad (2.11)$$

where we define

$$r_\pm = \frac{\beta \pm \sqrt{\beta^2 - 4\alpha\gamma}}{2\gamma} =: \frac{\beta \pm d}{\eta^2}$$

Integrating (2.11) with the terminal conditions $C(u, 0) = 0$ and $D(u, 0) = 0$ gives

$$D(u, \tau) = r_- \frac{1 - e^{-d\tau}}{1 - g\, e^{-d\tau}}$$

$$C(u, \tau) = \lambda \left\{ r_- \tau - \frac{2}{\eta^2} \log \left(\frac{1 - g\, e^{-d\tau}}{1 - g} \right) \right\} \qquad (2.12)$$

where we define

$$g := \frac{r_-}{r_+}$$

Taking the inverse transform using equation (2.8) and performing the complex integration carefully gives the final form of the pseudo-probabilities P_j in the form of an integral of a real-valued function.

$$P_j(x, v, \tau) = \frac{1}{2} + \frac{1}{\pi} \int_0^\infty du\, Re \left\{ \frac{\exp\{C_j(u, \tau)\, \bar{v} + D_j(u, \tau)\, v + i\, u\, x\}}{i\, u} \right\} \qquad (2.13)$$

This integration may be performed using standard numerical methods.

It is worth noting that taking derivatives of the Heston formula with respect to x or v in order to compute delta and vega is extremely straightforward because the functions $C(u, \tau)$ and $D(u, \tau)$ are independent of x and v.

A Digression: The Complex Logarithm in the Integration (2.13)

In Heston's original paper and in most other papers on the subject, $C(u, \tau)$ is written (almost) equivalently as

$$C(u, \tau) = \lambda \left\{ r_+ \tau - \frac{2}{\eta^2} \log \left(\frac{e^{+d\tau} - g}{1 - g} \right) \right\} \qquad (2.14)$$

The reason for the qualification "almost" is that this definition coincides with our previous one only if the imaginary part of the complex logarithm is chosen so that $C(u, \tau)$ is continuous with respect to u. It turns out that taking the principal value of the logarithm in (2.14) causes $C(u, \tau)$ to jump discontinuously each time the imaginary part of the argument of the logarithm crosses the negative real axis. The conventional resolution is to keep careful track of the winding number in the integration (2.13) so as to remain on the same Riemann sheet. This leads to practical implementation problems because standard numerical integration routines cannot be used. The paper of Kahl and Jäckel (2005) concerns itself with this problem and provides an ingenious resolution.

With *our* definition (2.12) of $C(u, \tau)$, however, as proved by Albrecher, Mayer, Schoutens, and Tistaert (2007), whenever the imaginary part of the argument of the logarithm is zero, the real part is positive; plotted in the complex plane, the argument of the logarithm never cuts the negative real axis. It follows that with our definition of $C(u, \tau)$, taking the principal value of the logarithm leads to a continuous integrand over the full range of integration.

DERIVATION OF THE HESTON CHARACTERISTIC FUNCTION

To anyone other than an option trader, it may seem perverse to first derive the option pricing formula and then impute the characteristic function: The reverse might appear more natural. However, in the context of understanding the volatility surface, option prices really are primary and it makes just as much sense for us to deduce the characteristic function from the option pricing formula as it does for us to deduce the risk-neutral density from option prices.

By definition, the characteristic function is given by

$$\phi_T(u) := \mathbb{E}[e^{iux_T} | x_t = 0]$$

The probability of the final log-stock price x_T being greater than the strike price is given by

$$\Pr(x_T > x) = P_0(x, v, \tau)$$
$$= \frac{1}{2} + \frac{1}{\pi} \int_0^\infty du \, Re \left\{ \frac{\exp\{C(u, \tau)\bar{v} + D(u, \tau)v + iux\}}{iu} \right\}$$

with $x = \log(S_t/K)$ and $\tau = T - t$. Let the log-strike k be defined by $k = \log(K/S_t) = -x$. Then, the probability density function $p(k)$ must be given by

$$p(k) = -\frac{\partial P_0}{\partial k}$$

$$= \frac{1}{2\pi} \int_{-\infty}^{\infty} du' \exp\{C(u', \tau)\bar{v} + D(u', \tau)v - iu'k\}$$

Then

$$\phi_T(u) = \int_{-\infty}^{\infty} dk \, p(k) \, e^{iuk}$$

$$= \frac{1}{2\pi} \int_{-\infty}^{\infty} du' \exp\{C(u', \tau)\bar{v} + D(u', \tau)v\} \int_{-\infty}^{\infty} du \, e^{i(u-u')k}$$

$$= \int_{-\infty}^{\infty} du' \exp\{C(u', \tau)\bar{v} + D(u', \tau)v\} \delta(u - u')$$

$$= \exp\{C(u, \tau)\bar{v} + D(u, \tau)v\} \tag{2.15}$$

SIMULATION OF THE HESTON PROCESS

Recall the Heston process

$$dS = \mu S dt + \sqrt{v} S \, dZ_1$$
$$dv = -\lambda(v - \bar{v}) \, dt + \eta \sqrt{v} \, dZ_2 \tag{2.16}$$

with

$$\langle dZ_1 \, dZ_2 \rangle = \rho \, dt$$

A simple Euler discretization of the variance process

$$v_{i+1} = v_i - \lambda (v_i - \bar{v}) \Delta t + \eta \sqrt{v_i} \sqrt{\Delta t} \, Z \tag{2.17}$$

with $Z \sim N(0, 1)$ may give rise to a negative variance. To deal with this problem, practitioners generally adopt one of two approaches: Either the absorbing assumption: if $v < 0$ then $v = 0$, or the reflecting assumption: if $v < 0$ then $v = -v$. In practice, with the parameter values that are required to fit equity index option prices, a huge number of time steps is required to achieve convergence with this discretization.

Milstein Discretization

It turns out to be possible to substantially alleviate the negative variance problem by implementing a Milstein discretization scheme.

Specifically, by going to one higher order in the Itô-Taylor expansion[*] of $v(t + \Delta t)$, we arrive at the following discretization of the variance process:

$$v_{i+1} = v_i - \lambda \, (v_i - \bar{v}) \, \Delta t + \eta \, \sqrt{v_i} \, \sqrt{\Delta t} \, Z + \frac{\eta^2}{4} \, \Delta t \, \left(Z^2 - 1 \right) \qquad (2.18)$$

This can be rewritten as

$$v_{i+1} = \left(\sqrt{v_i} + \frac{\eta}{2} \, \sqrt{\Delta t} \, Z \right)^2 - \lambda \, (v_i - \bar{v}) \, \Delta t - \frac{\eta^2}{4} \, \Delta t$$

We note that if $v_i = 0$ and $4 \lambda \bar{v} / \eta^2 > 1$, $v_{i+1} > 0$ indicating that the frequency of occurrence of negative variances should be substantially reduced. In practice, with typical parameters, even if $4 \lambda \bar{v} / \eta^2 < 1$, the frequency with which the process goes negative is substantially reduced relative to the Euler case.

As it is no more computationally expensive to implement the Milstein discretization (2.18) than it is to implement the Euler discretization (2.17), the Milstein discretization is always to be preferred. Also, the stock process should be discretized as

$$x_{i+1} = x_i - \frac{v_i}{2} \, \Delta t + \sqrt{v_i \, \Delta t} \, W$$

with $x_i := \log(S_i / S_0)$ and $W \sim N(0, 1)$, $\mathbb{E}[Z \, W] = \rho$; if we discretize the equation for the log-stock price x rather than the equation for the stock price S, there are no higher order corrections to the Euler discretization.

An Implicit Scheme   We follow Alfonsi (2005) and consider

$$v_{i+1} = v_i - \lambda \, (v_i - \bar{v}) \, \Delta t + \eta \, \sqrt{v_i} \, \sqrt{\Delta t} \, Z$$

$$= v_i - \lambda \, (v_{i+1} - \bar{v}) \, \Delta t + \eta \, \sqrt{v_{i+1}} \, \sqrt{\Delta t} \, Z$$

$$- \eta \, \left(\sqrt{v_{i+1}} - \sqrt{v_i} \right) \sqrt{\Delta t} \, Z + \text{higher order terms}$$

We note that

$$\sqrt{v_{i+1}} - \sqrt{v_i} = \frac{\eta}{2} \, \sqrt{\Delta t} \, Z + \text{higher order terms}$$

---

[*]See Chapter 5 of Kloeden and Platen (1992) for a discussion of Itô-Taylor expansions.

and substitute (noting that $\mathbb{E}[Z^2] = 1$) to obtain the implicit discretization

$$v_{i+1} = v_i - \lambda\,(v_{i+1} - \bar{v})\,\Delta t + \eta\,\sqrt{v_{i+1}}\,\sqrt{\Delta t}\,Z - \frac{\eta}{2}\,\Delta t \qquad (2.19)$$

Then $\sqrt{v_{i+1}}$ may be obtained as a root of the quadratic equation (2.19). Explicitly,

$$\sqrt{v_{i+1}} = \frac{\sqrt{4\,v_i + \Delta t\left[(\lambda\,\bar{v} - \eta^2/2)\,(1 + \lambda\,\Delta t) + \eta^2\,Z^2\right]} + \eta\,\sqrt{\Delta t}\,Z}{2\,(1 + \lambda\,\Delta t)}$$

If $2\,\lambda\,\bar{v}/\eta^2 > 1$, there is guaranteed to be a real root of this expression so variance is guaranteed to be positive. Otherwise, there's no guarantee and this discretization doesn't work.

Given that Heston parameters in practice often don't satisfy $2\,\lambda\,\bar{v}/\eta^2 > 1$, we are led to prefer the Milstein discretization, which is in any case simpler.

Sampling from the Exact Transition Law

As Paul Glasserman (2004) points out in his excellent book on Monte Carlo methods, the problem of negative variances may be avoided altogether by sampling from the exact transition law of the process. Broadie and Kaya (2004) show in detail how this may be done for the Heston process but their method turns out also to be very time consuming as it involves integration of a characteristic function expressed in terms of Bessel functions.

It is nevertheless instructive to follow their argument. The exact solution of (2.16) may be written as

$$S_t = S_0 \exp\left\{-\frac{1}{2}\int_0^t v_s\,ds + \rho\int_0^t \sqrt{v_s}\,dZ_s + \sqrt{1 - \rho^2}\int_0^t \sqrt{v_s}\,dZ_s^{\perp}\right\}$$

$$v_t = v_0 + \lambda\,\bar{v}\,t - \lambda\int_0^t v_s\,ds + \eta\int_0^t \sqrt{v_s}\,dZ_s$$

with

$$\langle dZ_s\,dZ_s^{\perp}\rangle = 0$$

The Broadie-Kaya simulation procedure is as follows:

- Generate a sample from the distribution of v_t given v_0.
- Generate a sample from the distribution of $\int_0^t v_s\,ds$ given v_t and v_0.

- Recover $\int_0^t \sqrt{v_s}\, dZ_s$ given $\int_0^t v_s\, ds$, v_t and v_0.
- Generate a sample from the distribution of S_t given $\int_0^t \sqrt{v_s}\, dZ_s$ and $\int_0^t v_s\, ds$.

Note that in the final step, the distribution of $\int_0^t \sqrt{v_s}\, dZ_s^\perp$ is normal with variance $\int_0^t v_s\, ds$ because $dZ_s^\perp$ and v_s are independent by construction.

Andersen and Brotherton-Ratcliffe (2001) suggest that processes like the square root variance process should be simulated by sampling from a distribution that is similar to the true distribution but not necessarily the same; this approximate distribution should have the same mean and variance as the true distribution.

Applying their suggested approach to simulating the Heston process, we would have to find the means and variances of $\int_0^t \sqrt{v_s}\, dZ_s$, $\int_0^t v_s\, ds$, v_t and v_0.

Why the Heston Model Is so Popular

From the above remarks on Monte Carlo simulation, the reader can get a sense of how computationally expensive it can be to get accurate values of options in a stochastic volatility model; numerical solution of the PDE is not much easier. The great difference between the Heston model and other (potentially more realistic) stochastic volatility models is the existence of a fast and easily implemented quasi-closed form solution for European options. This computational efficiency in the valuation of European options becomes critical when calibrating the model to known option prices.

As we shall see in subsequent chapters, although the dynamics of the Heston model are not realistic, with appropriate choices of parameters, all stochastic volatility models generate roughly the same shape of implied volatility surface and have roughly the same implications for the valuation of nonvanilla derivatives in the sense that they are all models of the joint process of the stock price and instantaneous variance. Given the relative cheapness of Heston computations, it's easy to see why the model is so popular.

CHAPTER 3

The Implied Volatility Surface

I n Chapter 1, we showed how to compute local volatilities from implied volatilities. In this chapter, we show how to get implied volatilities from local volatilities. Using the fact that local variance is a conditional expectation of instantaneous variance, we can estimate local volatilities generated by a given stochastic volatility model; implied volatilities then follow. Given a stochastic volatility model, we can then approximate the shape of the implied volatility surface.

Conversely, given the shape of an actual implied volatility surface, we find we can deduce some characteristics of the underlying process.

GETTING IMPLIED VOLATILITY FROM LOCAL VOLATILITIES

Model Calibration

For a model to be useful in practice, it needs to return (at least approximately) the current market prices of European options. That implies that we need to fit the parameters of our model (whether stochastic or local volatility model) to market implied volatilities. It is clearly easier to calibrate a model if we have a fast and accurate method for computing the prices of European options as a function of the model parameters. In the case of stochastic volatility, this consideration clearly favors models such as Heston that have such a solution; Mikhailov and Nögel (2003), for example, explain how to calibrate the Heston model to market data.

In the case of local volatility models, numerical methods are usually required to compute European option prices and that is one of the potential problems associated with their implementation. Brigo and Mercurio (2003) circumvent this problem by parameterizing the local volatility in such a way that the prices of European options are known in closed-form as superpositions of Black-Scholes-like solutions.

Yet again, we could work with the European option prices directly in a trinomial tree framework as in Derman, Kani, and Chriss (1996) or we could maximize relative entropy (of missing information) as in Avellaneda, Friedman, Holmes, and Samperi (1997). These methods are nonparametric (assuming actual option prices are used, not interpolated or extrapolated values); they may fail because of noise in the prices and the bid/offer spread.

Finally, we could parameterize the risk-neutral distributions as in Rubinstein (1998) or parameterize the implied volatility surface directly as in Shimko (1993) or Gatheral (2004). Although these approaches look straightforward given that we know from Chapter 1 how to get local volatility in terms of implied volatility, they are very difficult to implement in practice. The problem is that we don't have a complete implied volatility surface, we only have a few bids and offers per expiration. To apply a parametric method, we need to interpolate and extrapolate the known implied volatilities. It is very hard to do this without introducing arbitrage. The arbitrages to avoid are roughly speaking, negative vertical spreads, negative butterflies and negative calendar spreads (where the latter are carefully defined).

In what follows, we concentrate on the implied volatility structure of stochastic volatility models so as not to worry about the possibility of arbitrage, which is excluded from the outset.

First, we derive an expression for implied volatility in terms of local volatilities. In principle, this should allow us to investigate the shape of the implied volatility surface for any local volatility or stochastic volatility model because we know from equation (1.12) how to express local variance as an expectation of instantaneous variance in a stochastic volatility model.

Understanding Implied Volatility

In Chapter 1, we derived an expression (1.10) for local volatility in terms of implied volatility. An obvious direct approach might be to invert that expression and express implied volatility in terms of local volatility. However, this kind of direct attack on the problem doesn't yield any easy results in general although Berestycki, Busca, and Florent (2002) were able to invert (1.10) in the limit of zero time to expiration.

Instead, by exploiting the work of Dupire (1998), we derive a general path-integral representation of Black-Scholes implied variance. We start by assuming that the stock price S_t satisfies the SDE

$$\frac{dS_t}{S_t} = \mu_t dt + \sigma_t dZ_t$$

where the volatility σ_t may be random.

For fixed K and T, define the Black-Scholes gamma

$$\Gamma_{BS}(S_t, \overline{\sigma}(t)) := \frac{\partial^2}{\partial S_t^2} C_{BS}(S_t, K, \overline{\sigma}(t), T - t)$$

and further define the "Black-Scholes forward implied variance" function

$$v_{K,T}(t) = \frac{\mathbb{E}\left[\sigma_t^2 S_t^2 \Gamma_{BS}(S_t, \overline{\sigma}(t)) \,|\, \mathcal{F}_0\right]}{\mathbb{E}\left[S_t^2 \Gamma_{BS}(S_t, \overline{\sigma}(t)) \,|\, \mathcal{F}_0\right]} \tag{3.1}$$

where

$$\overline{\sigma}^2(t) := \frac{1}{T - t} \int_t^T v_{K,T}(u) \, du \tag{3.2}$$

Path-by-path, for any suitably smooth function $f(S_t, t)$ of the random stock price S_t and for any given realization $\{\sigma_t\}$ of the volatility process, the difference between the initial value and the final value of the function $f(S_t, t)$ is obtained by antidifferentiation. Then, applying Itô's lemma, we get

$$f(S_T, T) - f(S_0, 0) = \int_0^T df$$

$$= \int_0^T \left\{ \frac{\partial f}{\partial S_t} dS_t + \frac{\partial f}{\partial t} dt + \frac{\sigma_t^2}{2} S_t^2 \frac{\partial^2 f}{\partial S_t^2} dt \right\} \tag{3.3}$$

Under the usual assumptions, the nondiscounted value $C(S_0, K, T)$ of a call option is given by the expectation of the final payoff under the risk-neutral measure. Then, applying (3.3), we obtain:

$$C(S_0, K, T) = \mathbb{E}\left[(S_T - K)^+ \,|\, \mathcal{F}_0\right]$$

$$= \mathbb{E}\left[C_{BS}(S_T, K, \overline{\sigma}(T), 0) \,|\, \mathcal{F}_0\right]$$

$$= C_{BS}(S_0, K, \overline{\sigma}(0), T)$$

$$+ \mathbb{E}\left[\int_0^T \left\{ \frac{\partial C_{BS}}{\partial S_t} dS_t + \frac{\partial C_{BS}}{\partial t} dt + \frac{1}{2}\sigma_t^2 S_t^2 \frac{\partial^2 C_{BS}}{\partial S_t^2} dt \right\} \middle| \mathcal{F}_0 \right]$$

Now, of course, $C_{BS}(S_t, K, \overline{\sigma}(t), T - t)$ must satisfy the Black-Scholes equation (assuming zero interest rates and dividends) and from the definition of $\overline{\sigma}(t)$, we obtain:

$$\frac{\partial C_{BS}}{\partial t} = -\frac{1}{2} v_{K,T}(t) \, S_t^2 \frac{\partial^2 C_{BS}}{\partial S_t^2}$$

Using this equation to substitute for the time derivative $\frac{\partial C_{BS}}{\partial t}$, we obtain:

$$C(S_0, K, T) = C_{BS}(S_0, K, \overline{\sigma}(0), T)$$

$$+ \mathbb{E}\left[\int_0^T \left\{ \frac{\partial C_{BS}}{\partial S_t} dS_t + \frac{1}{2}\left\{\sigma_t^2 - \nu_{K,T}(t)\right\} S_t^2 \frac{\partial^2 C_{BS}}{\partial S_t^2} dt\right\}\middle| \mathcal{F}_0\right]$$

$$= C_{BS}(S_0, K, \overline{\sigma}(0), T)$$

$$+ \mathbb{E}\left[\int_0^T \frac{1}{2}\left\{\sigma_t^2 - \nu_{K,T}(t)\right\} S_t^2 \frac{\partial^2 C_{BS}}{\partial S_t^2} dt\middle| \mathcal{F}_0\right] \qquad (3.4)$$

where the second equality uses the fact that S_t is a martingale.

In words, the last term in equation (3.4) gives the expected realized profit on a sale of a call option at an implied volatility of $\overline{\sigma}$, delta-hedged using the deterministic forward variance function $\nu_{K,T}$ when the actual realized volatility is σ_t.

From the definition (3.2) of $\nu_{K,T}(t)$, we have that

$$\mathbb{E}\left[S_t^2 \Gamma_{BS}(S_t, \overline{\sigma}(t))\,|\mathcal{F}_0\right]\nu_{K,T}(t) = \mathbb{E}\left[\sigma_t^2 S_t^2 \Gamma_{BS}(S_t, \overline{\sigma}(t))\,|\mathcal{F}_0\right]$$

so the second term in equation (3.4) vanishes and from the definition of implied volatility, $\overline{\sigma}(0)$ is the Black-Scholes implied volatility at time 0 of the option with strike K and expiration T (*i.e.*, the Black-Scholes formula must give the market price of the option).

Explicitly,

$$\sigma_{BS}(K, T)^2 = \overline{\sigma}(0)^2 = \frac{1}{T}\int_0^T \frac{\mathbb{E}\left[\sigma_t^2 S_t^2 \Gamma_{BS}(S_t)\,|\mathcal{F}_0\right]}{\mathbb{E}\left[S_t^2 \Gamma_{BS}(S_t)\,|\mathcal{F}_0\right]} dt \qquad (3.5)$$

Equation (3.5) expresses implied variance as the time-integral of expected instantaneous variance σ_t^2 under some probability measure.

The interpretation of equation (3.5) is that to compute the Black-Scholes implied volatility of an option, we need to average the possible realized volatilities over all possible scenarios, in particular over all possible paths of the underlying stock. Each such scenario is weighted by the gamma of the option; the profitability of the delta hedger in any time interval is directly proportional to the gamma and the difference between "expected instantaneous variance" (or local variance) and realized instantaneous variance. In particular, at inception of the delta hedge, there is only one possible stock price (the then stock price) and only paths that end at the strike price need be included in the average because gamma elsewhere is precisely zero.

Following Lee (2005), we may rewrite (3.5) more elegantly as

$$\sigma_{BS}(K,T)^2 = \overline{\sigma}(0)^2 = \frac{1}{T} \int_0^T \mathbb{E}^{G_t}[\sigma_t^2]\, dt \tag{3.6}$$

thus interpreting the definition (3.1) of $v(t)$ as the expectation of σ_t^2 with respect to the probability measure $\mathbb{G}_t$ defined, relative to the pricing measure $\mathbb{P}$, by the Radon-Nikodym derivative

$$\frac{d\mathbb{G}_t}{d\mathbb{P}} := \frac{S_t^2\, \Gamma_{BS}(S_t, \overline{\sigma}(t))}{\mathbb{E}\left[S_t^2\, \Gamma_{BS}(S_t, \overline{\sigma}(t)) \,|\, \mathcal{F}_0\right]}$$

Note in passing that equations (3.1) and (3.5) are implicit because the gamma $\Gamma_{BS}(S_t)$ of the option depends on all the forward implied variances $v_{K,T}(t)$.

Special Case (Black-Scholes) Suppose $\sigma_t = \sigma(t)$, a function of t only. Then

$$v_{K,T}(t) = \frac{\mathbb{E}\left[\sigma(t)^2 S_t^2 \Gamma_{BS}(S_t) \,|\, \mathcal{F}_0\right]}{\mathbb{E}\left[S_t^2 \Gamma_{BS}(S_t) \,|\, \mathcal{F}_0\right]} = \sigma(t)^2$$

The forward implied variance $v_{K,T}(t)$ and the forward variance $\sigma(t)^2$ coincide. As expected, $v_{K,T}(t)$ has no dependence on the strike K or the option expiration T.

Interpretation In order to get better intuition for equation (3.1), first recall how to compute a risk-neutral expectation:

$$\mathbb{E}^P\left[f(S_t)\right] = \int dS_t\, p(S_t, t; S_0)\, f(S_t)$$

We get the risk-neutral pdf of the stock price at time t by taking the second derivative of the market price of European options with respect to strike price.

$$p(S_t, t; S_0) = \left. \frac{\partial^2 C(S_0, K, t)}{\partial K^2} \right|_{K=S_t}$$

Then from equation (3.6) we have

$$v_{K,T}(t) = \mathbb{E}^{G_t}\left[\sigma_t^2\right]$$

$$= \mathbb{E}^P\left[\sigma_t^2 \frac{d\mathbb{G}_t}{d\mathbb{P}}\right]$$

$$= \int dS_t \, q \, (S_t; S_0, K, T) \, \mathbb{E}^P \left[\sigma_t^2 | S_t \right]$$

$$= \int dS_t \, q \, (S_t; S_0, K, T) \, v_L(S_t, t) \qquad (3.7)$$

where we further define

$$q \, (S_t, t; S_0, K, T) := \frac{p \, (S_t, t; S_0) \, S_t^2 \, \Gamma_{BS}(S_t)}{\mathbb{E} \left[S_t^2 \, \Gamma_{BS}(S_t) \, | \mathcal{F}_0 \right]}$$

and $v_L(S_t, t) = \mathbb{E}^P \left[\sigma_t^2 | S_t \right]$ is the local variance.

We see that $q \, (S_t, t; S_0, K, T)$ looks like a Brownian Bridge density for the stock price: $p \, (S_t, t; S_0)$ has a delta function peak at S_0 at time 0 and $\Gamma_{BS}(S_t)$ has a delta function peak at K at expiration T.

For convenience in what follows, we now rewrite equation (3.7) in terms of $x_t := \log \, (S_t/S_0)$:

$$v_{K,T} \, (t) = \int dx_t \, q \, (x_t, t; x_T, T) \, v_L(x_t, t) \qquad (3.8)$$

Figure 3.1 shows how $q \, (x_t, t; x_T, T)$ looks in the case of a 1-year European option struck at 1.3 with a flat 20% volatility. We see that $q \, (x_t, t; x_T, T)$ peaks on a line, which we will denote by $\tilde{x}_t$, joining the stock price today with the strike price at expiration. Moreover, the density looks roughly symmetric around the peak. This suggests an expansion around the peak $\tilde{x}_t$, at which the derivative of $q \, (x_t, t; x_t, T)$ with respect to x_t is zero. Then we write

$$q \, (x_t, t; x_T, T) \approx q(\tilde{x}_t, t; x_T, T) + \frac{1}{2} \, (x_t - \tilde{x}_t)^2 \, \frac{\partial^2 q}{\partial x_t^2} \bigg|_{x_t = \tilde{x}_t} \qquad (3.9)$$

In practice, the local variance $v_L(x_t, t)$ is typically not so far from linear in x_t in the region where $q \, (x_t, t; x_T, T)$ is significant, so we may further write

$$v_L(x_t, t) \approx v_L(\tilde{x}_t, t) + (x_t - \tilde{x}_t) \, \frac{\partial v_L}{\partial x_t} \bigg|_{x_t = \tilde{x}_t} \qquad (3.10)$$

Substituting (3.9) and (3.10) into the integrand in equation (3.8) gives

$$v_{K,T} \, (t) \approx v_L(\tilde{x}_t, t)$$

and we may rewrite equation (3.5) as

$$\sigma_{BS}(K, T)^2 \approx \frac{1}{T} \int_0^T v_L(\tilde{x}_t) \, dt \qquad (3.11)$$

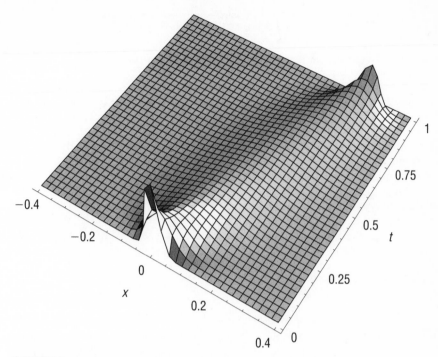

FIGURE 3.1 Graph of the pdf of x_t conditional on $x_T = \log(K)$ for a 1-year European option, strike 1.3 with current stock price = 1 and 20% volatility.

In words, equation (3.11) says that the Black-Scholes implied variance of an option with strike K is given approximately by the integral from valuation date $(t = 0)$ to the expiration date $(t = T)$ of the local variances along the path $\tilde{x}_t$ that maximizes the Brownian Bridge density $q\,(x_t, t; x_T, T)$.

Of course in practice, it's not easy to compute the path $\tilde{x}_t$. Nevertheless, we now have a very simple and intuitive picture for the meaning of Black-Scholes implied variance of a European option with a given strike and expiration: It is approximately the integral from today to expiration of local variances along the most probable path for the stock price conditional on the stock price at expiration being the strike price of the option.

LOCAL VOLATILITY IN THE HESTON MODEL

From equations (2.1) and (2.2) with $x_t := \log\,(S_t/K)$ and $\mu = 0$, we have

$$dx_t = -\frac{v_t}{2}dt + \sqrt{v_t}\,dZ_t$$

$$dv_t = -\lambda(v_t - \overline{v})dt + \rho\eta\sqrt{v_t}\,dZ_t + \sqrt{1 - \rho^2}\eta\sqrt{v_t}\,dW_t \qquad (3.12)$$

where dW_t and dZ_t are orthogonal. Eliminating $\sqrt{v_t}dZ_t$, we get

$$dv_t = -\lambda\,(v_t - \overline{v})\,dt + \rho\,\eta\left(dx_t + \frac{1}{2}v_t\,dt\right) + \sqrt{1 - \rho^2}\,\eta\,\sqrt{v_t}\,dW_t \quad (3.13)$$

Our strategy will be to compute local variances in the Heston model and then integrate local variance from valuation date to expiration date to approximate the BS implied variance using equation (3.11).

First, consider the unconditional expectation $\hat{v}_s$ of the instantaneous variance at time s. Solving equation (3.13) gives

$$\hat{v}_s = (v_0 - \overline{v})\,e^{-\lambda s} + \overline{v}$$

Then define the expected total variance to time t through the relation

$$\hat{w}_t := \int_0^t \hat{v}_s ds = (v_0 - \overline{v})\left\{\frac{1 - e^{-\lambda t}}{\lambda}\right\} + \overline{v}\,t$$

Finally, let $u_t := \mathbb{E}[v_t\,|x_T]$ be the expectation of the instantaneous variance at time t conditional on the final value x_T of x.

Ansatz

Ansatz means here, "Let's just suppose this were true so that we can proceed." Without loss of generality, assume $x_0 = 0$. Then

$$\mathbb{E}[x_s\,|x_T] = x_T\frac{\hat{w}_s}{\hat{w}_T}$$

where $\hat{w}_t := \int_0^t ds\,\hat{v}_s$ is the expected total variance to time t. To see that this ansatz is at least a plausible approximation, note that

$$\mathbb{E}\,(x_s) = \mathbb{E}(x_T)\frac{\hat{w}_s}{\hat{w}_T} = -\frac{\hat{w}_T}{2}\frac{\hat{w}_s}{\hat{w}_T} = -\frac{\hat{w}_s}{2}$$

In fact, if the process for x_t were a conventional Brownian Bridge process, the result would be true but in this case, the ansatz is only an approximation which is reasonable when $|x_T|$ is small (i.e. not too far from at-the-money).

Building on the ansatz, we may take the conditional expectation of (3.13) to get:

$$du_t = -\lambda(u_t - \overline{v})dt + \frac{\rho\eta}{2}u_t dt + \rho\eta\frac{x_T}{\hat{w}_T}d\hat{w}_t$$

$$+ \sqrt{1 - \rho^2}\eta\sqrt{v_t}\,\mathbb{E}[dW_t \,|x_T] \qquad (3.14)$$

If the dependence of dW_t on x_T is weak or if $\sqrt{1 - \rho^2}$ is very small, we may drop the last term to get

$$du_t \approx -\lambda'(u_t - \overline{v}')dt + \rho\eta\frac{x_T}{\hat{w}_T}\hat{v}_t dt$$

with $\lambda' = \lambda - \rho\eta/2$, $\overline{v}' = \overline{v}\lambda/\lambda'$. The solution to this equation is

$$u_T \approx \hat{v}'_T + \rho\eta\,\frac{x_T}{\hat{w}_T}\int_0^T \hat{v}_s\, e^{-\lambda'(T-s)}ds \qquad (3.15)$$

with $\hat{v}'_s := \left(v - \overline{v}'\right)e^{-\lambda's} + \overline{v}'$.

From equation (1.12), we know that the local variance $\sigma^2(K, T, S_0) = \mathbb{E}[v_T \,|S_T = K]$. Then, equation (3.15) gives us an approximate but surprisingly accurate formula for local variance within the Heston model (an extremely accurate approximation when $\rho = \pm 1$). We see that in the Heston model, local variance is approximately linear in $x = \log\left(\frac{F}{K}\right)$.

In summary, we have made two approximations: the ansatz and dropping the last term in equation (3.14). For reasonable parameters, equation (3.15) gives good intuition for the functional form of local variance and when $\rho = \pm 1$, as we will see in Chapter 4, it is almost exact. Peter Friz has shown that equation (3.15) is in fact exact to first order in η whether or not the ansatz holds or $\sqrt{1 - \rho^2}$ is small. Given this, equation (3.15) can also be shown to agree with the general perturbative expansions of Lewis (2000).

IMPLIED VOLATILITY IN THE HESTON MODEL

Now, to get implied variance in the Heston model, following our earlier explanation as summarized in equation (3.11), we need to integrate the Heston local variance along the most probable stock price path joining the initial stock price to the strike price at expiration (the one which maximizes the Brownian Bridge probability density).

Using our earlier notation, the Black-Scholes implied variance is given by

$$\sigma_{BS}(K, T)^2 \approx \frac{1}{T} \int_0^T \sigma_{\tilde{x}_t, t}^2 dt = \frac{1}{T} \int_0^T u_t(\tilde{x}_t) dt \qquad (3.16)$$

where $\{\tilde{x}_t\}$ is the most probable path (as defined earlier).

Recall that the Brownian Bridge density $q(x_t, t; x_T, T)$ is roughly symmetric and peaked around $\tilde{x}_t$, so $\mathbb{E}[x_t - \tilde{x}_t | x_T] \approx 0$. Applying the ansatz once again, we obtain

$$\tilde{x}_t = \mathbb{E}[\tilde{x}_t | x_T] = \mathbb{E}[\tilde{x}_t - x_t | x_T] + \mathbb{E}[x_t | x_T] \approx \frac{\hat{w}_t}{\hat{w}_T} x_T$$

We substitute this expression back into equations (3.15) and (3.16) to get

$$\sigma_{BS}(K, T)^2 \approx \frac{1}{T} \int_0^T u_t(\tilde{x}_t) dt$$

$$\approx \frac{1}{T} \int_0^T \hat{v}_t' dt + \rho\eta \, \frac{x_T}{\hat{w}_T} \frac{1}{T} \int_0^T dt \int_0^t \hat{v}_s \, e^{-\lambda'(t-s)} ds \qquad (3.17)$$

The Term Structure of Black-Scholes Implied Volatility in the Heston Model

The at-the-money term structure of BS implied variance in the Heston model is obtained by setting $x_T = 0$ in equation (3.17). Performing the integration explicitly gives

$$\sigma_{BS}(K, T)^2 \Big|_{K=F_T} \approx \frac{1}{T} \int_0^T \hat{v}_t' dt = \frac{1}{T} \int_0^T \left[(v - \bar{v}') e^{-\lambda' t} + \bar{v}' \right] dt$$

$$= (v - \bar{v}') \frac{1 - e^{-\lambda' T}}{\lambda' T} + \bar{v}' \qquad (3.18)$$

We see that in the Heston model, the at-the-money Black-Scholes implied variance

$$\sigma_{BS}(K, T)^2 \Big|_{K=F_T} \to v$$

(the instantaneous variance) as the time to expiration $T \to 0$ and as $T \to \infty$, the at-the-money Black-Scholes implied variance reverts to $\bar{v}'$.

The Black-Scholes Implied Volatility Skew in the Heston Model

It is possible (but not very illuminating) to integrate the second term of equation (3.17) explicitly. Even without doing that, we can see that the implied variance skew in the Heston model is approximately linear in the correlation ρ and the volatility of volatility η.

In the special case where $v_0 = \bar{v}$, the implied variance skew has a particularly simple form. Then $\hat{v}_s = \bar{v}$ and $\hat{w}_t = \bar{v}t$. The most probable path $\tilde{x}_t \approx \frac{t}{T}x_T$ is exactly a straight line in log-space between the initial stock price on valuation date and the strike price at expiration. Performing the integrations in equation (3.17) explicitly, we get

$$
\sigma_{BS}(K, T)^2 \approx \frac{\hat{w}'_T}{T} + \rho\eta\frac{x_T}{T^2}\int_0^T dt\,\frac{1}{T}\int_0^t e^{-\lambda'(t-s)}ds
$$

$$
= \frac{\hat{w}'_T}{T} + \rho\eta\,\frac{x_T}{\lambda'T}\left\{1 - \frac{\left(1 - e^{-\lambda'T}\right)}{\lambda'T}\right\} \qquad (3.19)
$$

From equation (3.19), we see that the implied variance skew $\frac{\partial}{\partial x_t}\sigma_{BS}$ $(K, T)^2$ is *independent* of the level of instantaneous variance v or long-term mean variance $\bar{v}$. In fact, this remains approximately true even when $v \neq \bar{v}$. It follows that we now have a fast way of calibrating the Heston model to observed implied volatility skews. Just two expirations would in principle allow us to determine λ' and the product $\rho\eta$. We can then fit the term structure of volatility to determine the long-term mean variance $\bar{v}$ and the instantaneous variance v_0. The curvature of the skew (not discussed here) would allow us to determine ρ and η separately.

We note that as we increase either the correlation ρ or the volatility of volatility η, the skew increases.

Also, the very short-dated skew is independent of λ and T:

$$
\frac{\partial}{\partial x_t}\sigma_{BS}(K, T)^2 = \rho\eta\,\frac{1}{\lambda'T}\left\{1 - \frac{\left(1 - e^{-\lambda'T}\right)}{\lambda'T}\right\} \rightarrow \frac{\rho\eta}{2}\,\text{ as }\,T \rightarrow 0
$$

and the long-dated skew is inversely proportional to T:

$$
\frac{\partial}{\partial x_t}\sigma_{BS}(K, T)^2 = \rho\eta\,\frac{1}{\lambda'T}\left\{1 - \frac{\left(1 - e^{-\lambda'T}\right)}{\lambda'T}\right\} \sim \frac{\rho\eta}{\lambda'T}\,\text{ as }\,T \rightarrow \infty
$$

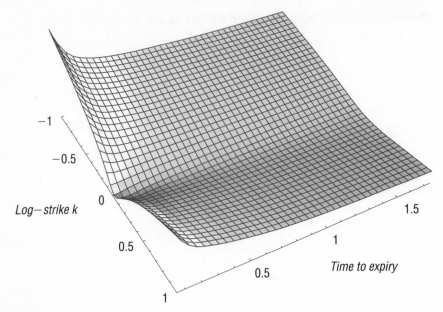

FIGURE 3.2   Graph of the SPX-implied volatility surface as of the close on September 15, 2005, the day before triple witching.

Finally, increasing η causes the curvature of the implied volatility skew (related to the kurtosis of the risk-neutral density) to increase, but we haven't shown that here.

THE SPX IMPLIED VOLATILITY SURFACE

Up to this point, we have concentrated on understanding the shape of the implied volatility surface as implied by a stochastic volatility model—in particular the Heston model. However, we still have no idea whether implied volatilities produced by the Heston model look like implied volatilities in the market.

To get a sense of what an actual implied volatility surface looks like, Figure 3.2 shows the surface resulting from a nonlinear (SVI) fit to observed implied variance as a function of k for each expiration on September 15, 2005, the day before the September triple-witching day.*

---

*A *triple-witching day* is a day on which both index option contracts and index futures contracts expire.

Another Digression: The SVI Parameterization

Gatheral (2004) presents the following "stochastic volatility inspired" (SVI) parameterization of the volatility smile. For each expiration, we write

$$\sigma_{BS}^2(k) = a + b \left\{ \rho(k - m) + \sqrt{(k - m)^2 + \sigma^2} \right\} \qquad (3.20)$$

where the coefficients a, b, ρ, σ, and m depend on the expiration.

This parameterization has a number of appealing properties, one of which is that it is relatively easy to eliminate calendar spread arbitrage. Thus, in an SVI fit, the functional form (3.20) is fitted to all expirations simultaneously subject to the constraint that there should be no arbitrage between expiration slices. Total implied variance may then be interpolated between slices to give a smooth surface. In this case, Stineman monotonic spline interpolation (Stineman 1980) was used.

Those readers skeptical as to whether the nice-looking surface in Figure 3.2 could really be a good fit may refer to the plot in Figure 3.3 to see fits to individual option bid and offer implied volatilities.

From the SVI fit, we impute the at-the-money forward variance levels and skews listed in Table 3.1. (Recall that by at-the-money skew, we mean $\frac{\partial}{\partial k}\sigma_{BS}(k, T)^2$ where k is the log-strike).

Skew is plotted as a function of time in Figure 3.4. Just looking at the pattern of the points, we would suspect that a simple functional form should be able to fit. However, the solid and dashed lines show the results of fitting the approximate formula

$$\rho \eta \frac{1}{\lambda' T} \left\{ 1 - \frac{\left(1 - e^{-\lambda' T}\right)}{\lambda' T} \right\} \qquad (3.21)$$

to the observed skews. The solid line takes all points into account; the dashed line drops the first three expirations from the fit. We can see that the fitting function is too stiff to fit the observed pattern of variance skews; there is no choice of λ' that will allow us to fit the skew observations. The fact that the observed variance skew increases significantly faster as $T \to 0$ than the skew implied by a stochastic volatility model may indicate that jumps need to be included in a complete model. We will explore this further in Chapter 5.

In Figure 3.5, we see that on this particular date, our simple formula fits the data pretty well. It should be emphasized that this is not always the case; in general, the term structure of volatility can be quite intricate at the

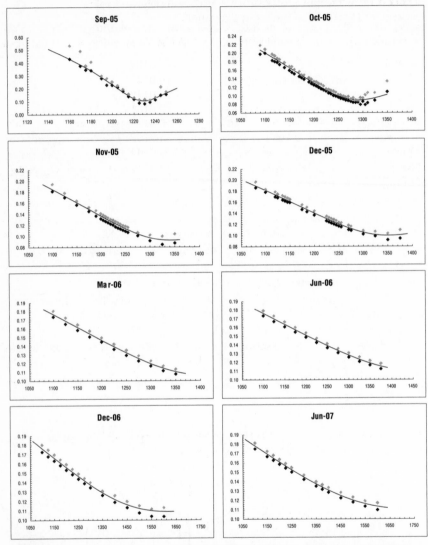

FIGURE 3.3 Plots of the SVI fits to SPX implied volatilities for each of the eight listed expirations as of the close on September 15, 2005. Strikes are on the x-axes and implied volatilities on the y-axes. The black and grey diamonds represent bid and offer volatilities respectively and the solid line is the SVI fit.

TABLE 3.1 At-the-money SPX variance levels and skews as of the close on September 15, 2005, the day before expiration.

Expiration	Time to Expiry	ATM Variance	ATM Skew
Sep-05	1 day	0.0109	−0.0955
Oct-05	1 month	0.0123	−0.1601
Nov-05	2 months	0.0149	−0.1372
Dec-05	3 months	0.0161	−0.1221
Mar-06	6 months	0.0183	−0.0945
Jun-06	9 months	0.0195	−0.0815
Dec-06	15 months	0.0209	−0.0679
Jun-07	21 months	0.0220	−0.0594

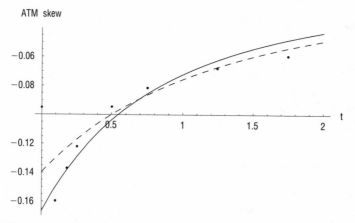

FIGURE 3.4 Graph of SPX ATM skew versus time to expiry. The solid line is a fit of the approximate skew formula (3.21) to all empirical skew points except the first; the dashed fit excludes the first three data points.

short end.

$$\sigma_{BS}(K, T)^2\Big|_{K=F_T} \approx (v - \bar{v}') \, \frac{1}{\lambda'T} \left\{ 1 - \frac{\left(1 - e^{-\lambda'T}\right)}{\lambda'T} \right\} + \bar{v}'$$

So, sometimes it's possible to fit the term structure of at-the-money volatility with a stochastic volatility model, but it's never possible to fit the term structure of the volatility skew for short expirations. That's one reason why practitioners prefer local volatility models: a stochastic volatility model with time-homogeneous parameters cannot fit market prices! Perhaps an extended stochastic volatility model with correlated jumps in stock price and

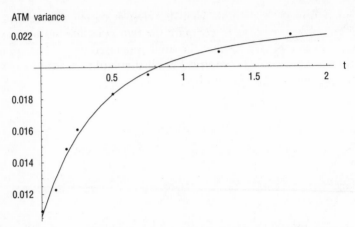

FIGURE 3.5 Graph of SPX ATM variance versus time to expiry. The solid line is a fit of the approximate ATM variance formula (3.18) to the empirical data.

volatility such as in Matytsin (1999) might fit better. But how would traders choose their input parameters? How would the SPX index book trader choose his volatility of volatility parameter—or worse, the correlation between jumps in stock price and jumps in volatility?

A Heston Fit to the Data

In Table 3.2, we list Heston parameters obtained from a fit to the September 15, 2005, SPX volatility surface graphed in Figure 3.2. On this particular date, the fitted Heston parameters were not so different from the BCC parameters. This is not usual and fitted Heston parameters in general move slowly over time. For example, the Heston volatility of volatility parameter η is found to increase as the general volatility level increases.

TABLE 3.2 Heston fit to the SPX surface as of the close on September 15, 2005.

v	0.0174
$\bar{v}$	0.0354
η	0.3877
ρ	−0.7165
λ	1.3253

A good way to judge how well the Heston model fits the empirical implied volatility surface is to compare the two volatility surfaces graphically. We see from Figure 3.6 that the smile generated by the Heston model is far too flat relative to the empirical implied volatility surface. For longer expirations, however, the fit isn't bad.

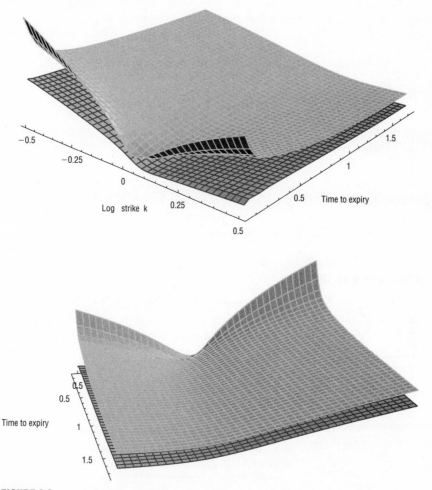

FIGURE 3.6 Comparison of the empirical SPX implied volatility surface with the Heston fit as of September 15, 2005. From the two views presented here, we can see that the Heston fit is pretty good for longer expirations but really not close for short expirations. The paler upper surface is the empirical SPX volatility surface and the darker lower one the Heston fit. The Heston fit surface has been shifted down by five volatility points for ease of visual comparison.

Final Remarks on SV Models and Fitting the Volatility Surface

It's quite clear from Figures 3.4 and 3.6 that the Heston model doesn't fit the observed implied volatility surface for short expirations, although the fit is not bad for longer expirations. Moreover, as we shall see in Chapter 7, all stochastic volatility models generate roughly the same shape of volatility surface. It follows that if we are looking for a model that fits options prices, we will need to look beyond stochastic volatility models.

CHAPTER 4

The Heston-Nandi Model

In Chapter 3, we derived approximate formulas for local and implied volatilities in the Heston model. In this chapter, we compute local and implied volatilities for a particular choice of Heston parameters for which equation (3.15) gives a very good approximation to the true local volatility. This provides us with a specific set of Heston parameters and local volatilities that we use in subsequent chapters to study the impact of modeling assumptions on the valuation of various kinds of options, confident that both local volatility and Heston models generate the same European option prices.

LOCAL VARIANCE IN THE HESTON-NANDI MODEL

Following the derivation in Chapter 3, we see that if $\rho = -1$, the formula presented for local variance should be pretty good (modulo some ansatz-related error). In this case, because $\rho = -1$, the Heston process is only one-factor and the SDE can be written as

$$dx = -\frac{v}{2}dt + \sqrt{v}\,dZ$$

$$dv = -\lambda\,(v - \bar{v})\,dt - \eta\,\sqrt{v}dZ$$

The choice $\rho = -1$ was originally studied by Heston and Nandi (1998) as the preference-free continuous time limit of a discrete GARCH option pricing model previously introduced by them. Their model was preference-free because there is only one source of randomness. So all volatility risk can be eliminated by appropriately delta hedging with stock; there is no volatility risk premium in this case.

Although the Heston model is only one factor in this special case, it is certainly not Markov in the stock price. That's because the instantaneous volatility is a deterministic function of the entire history of the stock price and in general, computing an expectation under the risk-neutral measure requires knowledge of the volatility. To see this clearly, we can rewrite the SDE for v as

$$dv = -\lambda' \, (v - \bar{v}') \, dt - \eta \, dx$$

with $\lambda' = \lambda + \eta/2$, $\bar{v}' = \bar{v}\lambda/\lambda'$. Note also that although zero instantaneous variance may be attainable depending on the value of the parameters, it can never be negative. In particular, local variance can never be negative.

From equation (3.11), local variance in this special case is given by

$$v_{loc}(x_T, T) = \hat{v}'_T - \eta \, \frac{x_T}{w_T} \int_0^T \hat{v}_s \, e^{-\lambda'(T-s)} ds$$

$$= (v - \bar{v}')e^{-\lambda'T} + \bar{v}' - \eta \, x_T \left\{ \frac{1 - e^{-\lambda'T}}{\lambda'T} \right\} \qquad (4.1)$$

The whole expression must be bounded below by zero—all stock prices above the critical stock price at which the local variance reaches zero are unattainable.

A NUMERICAL EXAMPLE

In order to assess the accuracy of the approximate local volatility formula (3.15), while also exploring some properties of the Heston-Nandi model, we fix Heston parameters as follows:

$$v = 0.04$$
$$\bar{v} = 0.04$$
$$\lambda = 10$$
$$\eta = 1$$
$$\rho = -1 \qquad (4.2)$$

We will use these parameters repeatedly in Heston computations throughout the rest of the book.

The Heston-Nandi Density

To get the Heston-Nandi probability density $p(k, T)$ for a given expiration T, we invert the Heston characteristic function $\phi_T(u)$,

$$p(k, T) = \frac{1}{2\pi} \int_{-\infty}^{+\infty} du\, \phi_T(u)\, e^{-iuk}$$

with

$$\phi_T(u) = \exp\{C(u, \tau)\, \bar{v} + D(u, \tau)\, v\}$$

from equation (2.15).

Computing $p(k, T)$ numerically with $T = 0.1$ years and the above parameters generates the plot shown in Figure 4.1. It's easy to see from this plot that stock prices above some critical stock price are unattainable in the Heston-Nandi model; there is a critical strike price above which call options have zero value. This observation alone makes the Heston-Nandi model look rather unrealistic.

Computation of Local Volatilities

From Chapter 3, local variance (the square of local volatility) is obtained from the Dupire equation (1.4) as the ratio of a calendar spread (time derivative) to a butterfly (probability density). We have already computed the density $p(k, T)$ so it only remains for us to compute the calendar spread. This we may do by differentiating the Heston call value with respect to the time to expiration τ. From equation (2.5),

$$\partial_\tau C(x, v, \tau) = K\left\{e^x\, \partial_\tau P_1(x, v, \tau) - \partial_\tau P_0(x, v, \tau)\right\}$$

with the $P_j(\cdot)$ are from equation (2.13).

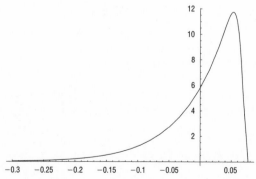

FIGURE 4.1 The probability density for the Heston-Nandi model with our parameters and expiration $T = 0.1$.

Inverting equation (1.4) then leads to

$$v_{loc}(x_t, \tau) = 2 \frac{\partial_\tau c(x_t, \tau)}{p(k, \tau)} \qquad (4.3)$$

with

$$c(x, \tau) := \frac{C(x, v, \tau)}{K}$$

Figure 4.2 shows the results of computing local volatility in the Heston-Nandi model using the exact (but possibly numerically inaccurate) formula (4.1) and the approximate (but numerically accurate) formula (4.3).

Computation of Implied Volatilities

The reader may or may not be convinced by the close agreement between the approximate and exact local volatilities plotted in Figure 4.2. For one thing, it's unclear whether errors at low strikes are due to the inaccuracy of the approximation or numerical inaccuracy in the computation of the exact local volatilities.

The proof of the pudding is in the eating: All we need is for the prices of European options to agree. We therefore compute European option prices using the Heston formula (2.13) and again by solving the local volatility valuation equation numerically* with local volatilities given by equation (4.1). Explicitly, the numerical PDE to be solved for an option with strike K and expiration T is

$$\frac{\partial V}{\partial t} + \frac{1}{2} v(S, t) S^2 \frac{\partial^2 V}{\partial S^2} = 0$$

subject to the boundary condition $V(S_T, T) = (S_T - K)^+$ where, from equation (4.1),

$$v(S, t) = (v - \bar{v}')e^{-\lambda'T} + \bar{v}' - \eta \, \log(S/S_0) \left\{ \frac{1 - e^{-\lambda'T}}{\lambda'T} \right\}$$

In Figure 4.3, we see again that agreement is very close.

---

*The solution of option pricing problems using numerical PDE techniques is covered extensively in Tavella and Randall (2000).

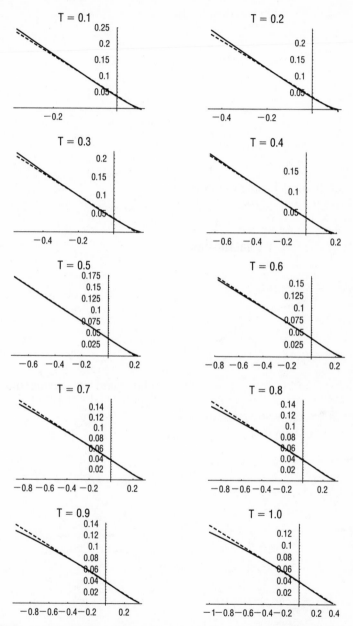

FIGURE 4.2 Comparison of approximate formulas with direct numerical computation of Heston local variance. For each expiration T, the solid line is the numerical computation and the dashed line is the approximate formula.

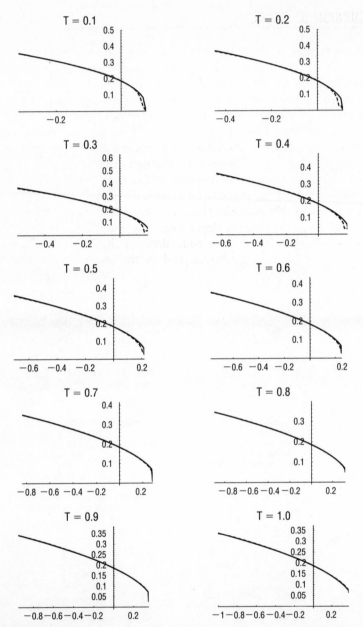

FIGURE 4.3 Comparison of European implied volatilities from application of the Heston formula (2.13) and from a numerical PDE computation using the local volatilities given by the approximate formula (4.1). For each expiration T, the solid line is the numerical computation and the dashed line is the approximate formula.

DISCUSSION OF RESULTS

From the results of our computation, we can see that the local volatility model and the stochastic volatility model price European options almost identically. Thus we have created a toy set of market parameters that will allow us to compare the effects of stochastic volatility and local volatility assumptions on the valuation of various claims, confident that European options are almost identically priced under both sets of assumptions. An additional implicit (but reasonable) assumption will be that when we make such a comparison, any difference in valuation can be primarily ascribed to the difference in dynamical assumptions rather than to this special choice of parameters than makes computations particularly easy.

We note too that both the Heston-Nandi model and its local volatility equivalent are single-factor, depending only on stock prices. However, the two models are clearly not equivalent: in the local volatility model, volatilities are known in advance and in the stochastic volatility case, volatilities are uncertain. The consequences of this fundamental difference between the two models will become clear as we proceed to value various exotic options in succeeding chapters.

In other words, to value an option, it's not enough just to fit all the European option prices, we also need to assume some specific dynamics for the underlying.

CHAPTER 5

Adding Jumps

I n this chapter, we first explain why it is that jumps need to be modeled. Then we show how they are conventionally modeled. We will see that introducing jumps has very little effect on the shape of the volatility surface for longer-dated options; the impact on the shape of the volatility surface is all at the short-expiration end. In passing, we derive explicit characteristic functions for the popular SVJ and SVJJ models. We will see in particular that the SVJ model succeeds in generating a volatility surface that has most of the observed features of the empirical surface with fewer parameters than the SVJJ model.

WHY JUMPS ARE NEEDED

In Chapter 3, we indicated the possibility that jumps might explain why the skew is so steep for very short expirations and why the very short-dated term structure of skew is inconsistent with any stochastic volatility model. Another indication that jumps might be necessary to explain the volatility surface comes from Table 5.1. There, we see that there is a 5-cent bid for a 1,160 put which is over 67 points out-of-the-money expiring the following morning.* Historically, about 40% of the variance of SPX is from overnight moves and the at-the-money volatility at the time was about 10%. With these parameters, a 67 point move corresponds to around 13.7 standard deviations. The probability of a normally distributed variable making such a move is zero (to about 40 decimal places). And these 5-cent bids are only bids; one might suppose that actual trades would take place somewhere between the bid and the offer. Similarly, there is a 5-cent bid for a call struck at 1,250, about 23 points out-of-the-money. That's only about 4.7

---

*Recall that the final payoff of SPX options is set at the opening of trading on the following day (September 16 in this case).

TABLE 5.1 September 2005 expiration option prices as of the close on September 15, 2005. Triple witching is the following day. SPX is trading at 1227.73.

Strike	Call Bid	Call Ask	Put Bid	Put Ask
1160	66.70	68.70	0.05	0.25
1170	56.70	58.70	0.05	0.35
1175	51.70	53.70	0.05	0.10
1180	46.70	48.70	0.10	0.30
1190	36.70	38.70	0.10	0.15
1195	31.70	33.70	0.05	0.20
1200	26.70	28.70	0.15	0.25
1205	21.70	23.70	0.25	0.30
1210	16.80	18.60	0.30	0.40
1215	11.90	13.70	0.30	0.45
1220	8.00	8.80	0.65	0.75
1225	3.90	4.20	1.10	1.90
1230	1.50	2.00	2.80	4.20
1235	0.35	0.50	6.70	8.30
1240	0.15	0.25	11.40	13.20
1245	0.15	0.70	16.40	18.00
1250	0.05	0.10	21.30	22.70

standard deviations; but even the probability of a normally distributed variable making that much smaller move is just over one in a million. Diffusions just can't generate the size of moves over very short timescales that would be able to generate any value for such options.

High bids for options that would require an extreme move to end up in-the-money are just another manifestation of the extreme short-end smile in the SPX market just prior to expiration. From the perspective of a trader, the explanation is straightforward: Large moves do sometimes occur and it makes economic sense to bid for out-of-the-money options—at the very least to cover existing risk.

To make this concrete, in Figure 5.1, we superimpose observed implied volatilities with the implied volatility smile generated by the Heston model with Sep05 SPX parameters from Table 3.1.* We note in particular that the Heston smile is flat and completely inconsistent with the empirically observed smile.

On reflection, it is easy to see why extreme short-end skews are incompatible with stochastic volatility; if the underlying process is a diffusion and volatility of volatility is reasonable, volatility should be near constant on a

---

*For details of the SVI parameterization of the volatility smile see Gatheral (2004).

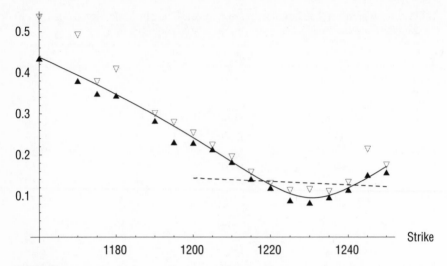

FIGURE 5.1   Graph of the September 16, 2005, expiration volatility smile as of the close on September 15, 2005. SPX is trading at 1227.73. Triangles represent bids and offers. The solid line is a nonlinear (SVI) fit to the data. The dashed line represents the Heston skew with Sep05 SPX parameters.

very short timescale. Then returns should be roughly normally distributed and the skew should be quite flat.

JUMP DIFFUSION

Derivation of the Valuation Equation

As in Wilmott (2000), we assume the stock price follows the SDE

$$dS = \mu S\, dt + \sigma S\, dZ + (J - 1)S\, dq \tag{5.1}$$

where the Poisson process

$$dq = \begin{cases} 0 & \text{with probability } 1 - \lambda(t)\, dt \\ 1 & \text{with probability } \lambda(t)\, dt \end{cases}$$

When $dq = 1$, the process jumps from S to JS. We assume that the Poisson process dq and the Brownian motion dZ are independent.

As in the stochastic volatility case, we derive a valuation equation by considering the hedging of a contingent claim. We make the (unrealistic) assumption at this stage that the jump size J is known in advance.

Whereas in the stochastic volatility case, the second risk factor to be hedged was the random volatility, in this case, the second factor is the jump. So once again, we set up a portfolio Π containing the option being priced whose value we denote by $V(S, v, t)$, a quantity $-\Delta$ of the stock and a quantity $-\Delta_1$ of another asset whose value V_1 also depends on the jump.

We have

$$\Pi = V - \Delta S - \Delta_1 V_1$$

The change in this portfolio in the time interval dt is given by

$$
\begin{aligned}
d\Pi = &\left\{ \frac{\partial V}{\partial t} + \frac{1}{2}\sigma^2 S^2 \frac{\partial^2 V}{\partial S^2} \right\} dt - \Delta_1 \left\{ \frac{\partial V_1}{\partial t} + \frac{1}{2}\sigma^2 S^2 \frac{\partial^2 V_1}{\partial S^2} \right\} dt \\
&+ \left\{ \frac{\partial V}{\partial S} - \Delta_1 \frac{\partial V_1}{\partial S} - \Delta \right\} dS^c \\
&+ \left\{ V(JS, t) - V(S, t) - \Delta_1(V_1(JS, t) - V_1(S, t)) - \Delta(J - 1)S \right\} dq
\end{aligned}
$$

where $S^c(t)$ is the continuous part of $S(t)$ (adding back all the jumps that occurred up to time t).

To make the portfolio instantaneously risk free, we must choose

$$\frac{\partial V}{\partial S} - \Delta_1 \frac{\partial V_1}{\partial S} - \Delta = 0$$

to eliminate dS terms, and

$$V(JS, t) - V(S, t) - \Delta_1(V_1(JS, t) - V_1(S, t)) - \Delta(J - 1)S = 0$$

to eliminate dq terms. This leaves us with

$$
\begin{aligned}
d\Pi &= \left\{ \frac{\partial V}{\partial t} + \frac{1}{2}\sigma^2 S^2 \frac{\partial^2 V}{\partial S^2} \right\} dt - \Delta_1 \left\{ \frac{\partial V_1}{\partial t} + \frac{1}{2}\sigma^2 S^2 \frac{\partial^2 V_1}{\partial S^2} \right\} dt \\
&= r\,\Pi\, dt \\
&= r(V - \Delta S - \Delta_1 V_1)\, dt
\end{aligned}
$$

where we have used the fact that the return on a risk-free portfolio must equal the risk-free rate r which we will assume to be deterministic for our purposes. Collecting all V terms on the left-hand side and all V_1 terms on the right-hand side, we get

$$\frac{\frac{\partial V}{\partial t} + \frac{1}{2}\sigma^2 S^2 \frac{\partial^2 V}{\partial S^2} + rS\frac{\partial V}{\partial S} - rV}{\delta V - (J-1)S\frac{\partial V}{\partial S}} = \frac{\frac{\partial V_1}{\partial t} + \frac{1}{2}\sigma^2 S^2 \frac{\partial^2 V_1}{\partial S^2} + rS\frac{\partial V_1}{\partial S} - rV_1}{\delta V_1 - (J-1)S\frac{\partial V_1}{\partial S}}$$

where we have defined $\delta V := V(JS, t) - V(S, t)$.

Continuing exactly as in the stochastic volatility case, the left-hand side is a function of V only and the right-hand side is a function of V_1 only. The only way that this can be is for both sides to be equal to some function of the independent variables S and t, which we will suggestively denote by $-\lambda$. We deduce that

$$\frac{\partial V}{\partial t} + \frac{1}{2}\sigma^2 S^2 \frac{\partial^2 V}{\partial S^2} + rS\frac{\partial V}{\partial S} - rV$$
$$+ \lambda(S, t)\left\{ V(JS, t) - V(S, t) - (J-1)S\frac{\partial V}{\partial S} \right\} = 0 \qquad (5.2)$$

To interpret $\lambda(S, t)$, consider the value P of an asset that pays \$1 at time T if there is no jump and zero otherwise. Our assumption that the jump process is independent of the stock price process implies that

$$\frac{\partial P}{\partial S} = 0$$

Also, we must have $P(JS, t) = 0$. Substituting into equation (5.2) gives

$$\frac{\partial P}{\partial t} - rP - \lambda(S, t)P = 0$$

Since (by assumption) P is independent of S, so must λ be and the solution is $P(t) = \exp\left\{ -\int_t^T (r + \lambda(t')) \, dt' \right\}$. We immediately recognize $\lambda(t)$ as the hazard rate of the Poisson process (the *pseudo-probability* per unit time that a jump occurs). We emphasize pseudo-probability because this is in no sense the actual probability (whatever that means) that a jump will occur. It is the value today of a financial asset.

Uncertain Jump Size

To derive equation (5.2), we assumed that we knew in advance what the jump size would be. Of course this is neither realistic nor practical. Jump diffusion models typically specify a distribution of jump sizes. How would this change equation (5.2)?

It is easy to see that adding another jump with a different size would require one more hedging asset in the replication argument. Allowing the jump size to be any real number with some distribution would require an infinite number of hedging assets. We see that in this case, the replication argument falls apart: Such jump diffusion models have no replicating hedge.

This is the major drawback of jump diffusion models. There is no replicating portfolio and so there is no self-financing hedge even in the limit of continuous trading. However, looking on the bright side, if we believe in jumps (as we must given the empirical evidence), options are no longer redundant assets that may be replicated using stocks and bonds and by extension, option traders can be seen to have genuine social value.

To extend equation (5.2) to the case of jumps of uncertain size, we assume that the risk-neutral process is still jump diffusion with jumps independent of the stock price. Under the risk-neutral measure, the expected return of any asset is the risk-free rate. Taking expectations of equation (5.1), we find that

$$\mathbb{E}[dS] = r\,S\,dt = \mu\,S\,dt + \mathbb{E}[J-1]\,S\,\lambda(t)\,dt$$

It follows that the risk-neutral drift is given by $\mu = r + \mu_J$ with

$$\mu_J = -\lambda(t)\,\mathbb{E}[J-1]$$

Just as in the derivation of the Black-Scholes equation, we must have $\mathbb{E}[dV] = r\,V\,dt$. Applying Itô's lemma and taking expectations under the risk-neutral measure give

$$\mathbb{E}[dV] = r\,V\,dt$$

$$= \left\{ \frac{\partial V}{\partial t} + r\,S\,\frac{\partial V}{\partial S} + \frac{1}{2}\sigma^2\,S^2\,\frac{\partial^2 V}{\partial S^2} \right\} dt$$

$$+ \lambda(t)\,\mathbb{E}[V(JS,t) - V(S)]\,dt + \mu_J\,S\,\frac{\partial V}{\partial S}\,dt$$

Rearranging, we obtain the following equation for valuing financial assets under jump diffusion:

$$\frac{\partial V}{\partial t} + \frac{1}{2}\sigma^2\,S^2\,\frac{\partial^2 V}{\partial S^2} + r\,S\,\frac{\partial V}{\partial S} - r\,V$$

$$+ \lambda(t)\left\{ \mathbb{E}\left[V(JS,t) - V(S,t)\right] - \mathbb{E}[J-1]\,S\,\frac{\partial V}{\partial S} \right\} = 0 \qquad (5.3)$$

Once again for emphasis, the expectations in equation (5.3) are under the risk-neutral measure. In order to value derivative assets, we concern ourselves only with the values that the market assigns to claims that pay in the event of a jump; actual probabilities don't enter at all.

CHARACTERISTIC FUNCTION METHODS

Unlike the partial differential equations (PDEs) we are used to solving in derivatives valuation problems, equation (5.3) is an example of a partial integro-differential equation (PIDE). The integration over all possible jump-sizes introduces nonlocality. Such equations can be solved using extensions of numerical PDE techniques but the most natural approach is to use Fourier transform (characteristic function) methods.

First, we review Lévy processes.

Lévy Processes

With constant hazard rate λ, the logarithmic version of the jump diffusion process (5.1) for the underlying asset is an example of a Lévy process.

Definition *A Lévy process is a continuous in probability, càdlàg stochastic process $x(t)$, $t > 0$ with independent and stationary increments and $x(0) = 0$.*

It turns out that any Lévy process can be expressed as the sum of a linear drift term, a Brownian motion, and a jump process. This plus the independent increment property leads directly to the following representation for the characteristic function.

The Lévy-Khintchine Representation If x_t is a Lévy process, and if the Lévy density $\mu(\chi)$ is suitably well behaved at the origin, its characteristic function $\phi_T(u) := \mathbb{E}\left[e^{iux_T}\right]$ has the representation

$$\phi_T(u) = \exp\left\{ iu\omega T - \frac{1}{2}u^2\sigma^2 T + T \int \left[e^{iu\chi} - 1\right]\mu(\chi)\,d\chi \right\} \qquad (5.4)$$

To get the drift parameter ω, we impose that the risk-neutral expectation of the stock price be the forward price. With our current assumption of zero interest rates and dividends, this translates to imposing that

$$\phi_T(-i) = \mathbb{E}\left[e^{x_T}\right] = 1$$

Here, $\int \mu(\chi)\,d\chi = \lambda$, the Poisson intensity or mean jump arrival rate, also known as the *hazard* rate.

Examples of Characteristic Functions for Specific Processes

Before proceeding to solve equation (5.3) for a particular specification of the jump process, we exhibit some examples of characteristic functions for processes with which we are already familiar.

Example 1: Black-Scholes The characteristic function for a exponential Brownian motion with volatility σ is given by

$$\phi_T(u) = \mathbb{E}\left[e^{iux_T}\right] = \exp\left\{-\frac{1}{2}u(u+i)\sigma^2 T\right\}$$

We can get this result by performing the integration explicitly or directly from the Lévy-Khintchine representation.

Example 2: Heston The Heston process is very path-dependent; increments are far from independent and it is not a Lévy process. However, we have already computed its characteristic function. From Chapter 2, we see that the characteristic function of the Heston process is given by (2.15)

$$\phi_T(u) = \exp\left\{C(u,T)\,\bar{v} + D(u,T)\,v\right\}$$

with $C(u,T)$ and $D(u,T)$ as defined there.

Example 3: Merton's Jump Diffusion Model Finally, this is the case we are really interested in. The jump-size J is assumed to be lognormally distributed with mean log-jump α and standard deviation δ so that the stock price follows the SDE

$$dS = \mu S\,dt + \sigma S\,dZ + (e^{\alpha+\delta\epsilon} - 1)S\,dq$$

with $\epsilon \sim N(0,1)$. Then

$$\mu(\chi) = \frac{\lambda}{\sqrt{2\pi\delta^2}}\exp\left\{-\frac{(\chi-\alpha)^2}{2\delta^2}\right\}$$

By applying the Lévy-Khintchine representation (5.4), we see that the characteristic function is given by

$$\phi_T(u) = \exp\left\{iu\omega T - \frac{1}{2}u^2\sigma^2 T + T\int\left[e^{iu\chi} - 1\right]\frac{\lambda}{\sqrt{2\pi\delta^2}}\right.$$
$$\left. \exp\left\{-\frac{(\chi-\alpha)^2}{2\delta^2}\right\}d\chi\right\}$$
$$= \exp\left\{iu\omega T - \frac{1}{2}u^2\sigma^2 T + \lambda T\left(e^{iu\alpha - u^2\delta^2/2} - 1\right)\right\} \qquad (5.5)$$

To get ω, we impose $\phi_T(-i) = 1$ so that

$$\exp\left\{\omega T + \frac{1}{2}\sigma^2 T + \lambda T\left(e^{\alpha+\delta^2/2} - 1\right)\right\} = 1$$

which gives

$$\omega = -\frac{1}{2}\sigma^2 - \lambda\left(e^{\alpha+\delta^2/2} - 1\right)$$

Unsurprisingly, we get the lognormal case back when we set $\alpha = \delta = 0$.

Alternatively, we can get the characteristic function for jump diffusion directly by substituting $\phi_T(u) = e^{\psi(u)T}$ into equation (5.3). With $y \sim N(\alpha, \delta)$, we obtain

$$\psi(u) = -\frac{1}{2}u(u+i)\sigma^2 - \lambda\left\{\mathbb{E}\left[e^{iuy} - 1\right] + iu\,\mathbb{E}\left[e^y - 1\right]\right\}$$

$$= -\frac{1}{2}u(u+i)\sigma^2 - \lambda\left\{\left(e^{iu\alpha - u^2\delta^2/2} - 1\right) + iu\left(e^{\alpha+\delta^2/2} - 1\right)\right\}$$

which gives an expression for $\phi_T(u)$ identical to the one already derived in equation (5.5).

Computing Option Prices from the Characteristic Function

It turns out (see Carr and Madan (1999) and Lewis (2000)) that it is quite straightforward to get option prices by inverting the characteristic function of a given stochastic process if it is known in closed form.

The formula we will use is a special case of formula (2.10) of Lewis. As usual, we assume zero interest rates and dividends:

$$C(S, K, T) = S - \sqrt{SK}\frac{1}{\pi}\int_0^\infty \frac{du}{u^2 + \frac{1}{4}}\,\text{Re}\left[e^{-iuk}\phi_T\left(u - i/2\right)\right] \qquad (5.6)$$

with $k = \log\left(\frac{K}{S}\right)$. We now proceed to prove this formula.

Proof of (5.6)

A covered call position has the payoff $\min[S_T, K]$ where S_T is the stock price at time T and K is the strike price of the call. Consider the Fourier transform of this covered call position $G(k, \tau)$ with respect to the log-strike

$k := \log(K/F)$ defined by

$$\hat{G}(u, \tau) = \int_{-\infty}^{\infty} e^{iuk} G(k, \tau) \, dx$$

Denoting the current time by t and expiration by T, and setting interest rates and dividends to zero as usual, we have that

$$\frac{1}{S}\hat{G}(u, T - t) = \int_{-\infty}^{\infty} e^{iuk}\mathbb{E}\left[\min[e^{x_T}, e^k)^+]|x_t = 0\right] dk$$

$$= \mathbb{E}\left[\int_{-\infty}^{\infty} e^{iuk} \min[e^{x_T}, e^k)^+]\, dk \,\bigg|\, x_t = 0\right]$$

$$= \mathbb{E}\left[\int_{-\infty}^{x_T} e^{iuk} e^k \, dk + \int_{x_T}^{\infty} e^{iuk} e^{x_T}\, dk \,\bigg|\, x_t = 0\right]$$

$$= \mathbb{E}\left[\frac{e^{(1+iu)x_T}}{1 + iu} - \frac{e^{(1+iu)x_T}}{iu}\,\bigg|\, x_t = 0\right] \text{ only if } 0 < \text{Im}[u] < 1!$$

$$= \frac{1}{u(u - i)}\mathbb{E}\left[e^{(1+iu)x_T}\,\big|\, x_t = 0\right]$$

$$= \frac{1}{u(u - i)}\,\phi_T(u - i)$$

by definition of the characteristic function $\phi_T(u)$. Note that the transform of the covered call value exists only if $0 < \text{Im}[u] < 1$. It is easy to see that this derivation would go through pretty much as above with other payoffs though it is key to note that the region where the transform exists depends on the payoff.

To get the call price in terms of the characteristic function, we express it in terms of the covered call and invert the Fourier transform, integrating along the line $\text{Im}[u] = 1/2$.* Then

$$C(S, K, T) = S - S\frac{1}{2\pi}\int_{-\infty+i/2}^{\infty+i/2} \frac{du}{u(u - i)}\,\phi_T(u - i)\, e^{-iku}$$

$$= S - S\frac{1}{2\pi}\int_{-\infty}^{\infty} \frac{du}{(u + i/2)(u - i/2)}\,\phi_T(u - i/2)\, e^{-ik(u+i/2)}$$

---

*That's why we chose to express the call in terms of the covered call whose transform exists in this region. Alternatively, we could have used the transform of the call price and Cauchy's Residue Theorem to do the inversion.

$$= S - \sqrt{SK}\frac{1}{\pi}\int_0^\infty \frac{du}{u^2 + \frac{1}{4}} \operatorname{Re}\left[e^{-iuk}\phi_T\left(u - i/2\right)\right]$$

with $k = \log\left(\frac{K}{S}\right)$.

Computing Implied Volatility

Equation (5.6) allows us to derive an elegant implicit expression for the Black-Scholes implied volatility of an option in any model for which the characteristic function is known.

Substituting the characteristic function for the Black-Scholes process into (5.6) gives

$$C_{BS}(S, K, T) = S - \sqrt{SK}\frac{1}{\pi}\int_0^\infty \frac{du}{u^2 + \frac{1}{4}} \operatorname{Re}\left[e^{-iuk}e^{-\frac{1}{2}\left(u^2 + \frac{1}{4}\right)\sigma_{BS}^2 T}\right]$$

Then, from the definition of implied volatility, we must have

$$\int_0^\infty \frac{du}{u^2 + \frac{1}{4}} \operatorname{Re}\left[e^{-iuk}\left(\phi_T\left(u - i/2\right) - e^{-\frac{1}{2}\left(u^2 + \frac{1}{4}\right)\sigma_{BS}^2 T}\right)\right] = 0 \qquad (5.7)$$

Equation (5.7) gives us a simple but implicit relationship between the implied volatility surface and the characteristic function of the underlying stock process. In particular, we may efficiently compute the structure of at-the-money implied volatility and the at-the-money volatility skew in terms of the characteristic function (at least numerically) without having to explicitly compute option prices.

Computing the At-the-Money Volatility Skew

Assume ϕ_T does not depend on spot S and hence not on k. (This is the case in all examples we have in mind.) Then differentiating (5.7) with respect to k and evaluating at $k = 0$ give

$$\int_0^\infty du \left\{\frac{u \operatorname{Im}[\phi_T(u - i/2)]}{u^2 + \frac{1}{4}} + \frac{1}{2}\left.\frac{\partial w_{BS}}{\partial k}\right|_{k=0} e^{-\frac{1}{2}\left(u^2 + \frac{1}{4}\right)w_{BS}(0,T)}\right\} = 0$$

Then, integrating the second term explicitly, we get

$$\left.\frac{\partial \sigma_{BS}}{\partial k}\right|_{k=0} = -e^{\frac{\sigma_{BS}^2 T}{8}}\sqrt{\frac{2}{\pi}}\frac{1}{\sqrt{T}}\int_0^\infty du \frac{u \operatorname{Im}[\phi_T(u - i/2)]}{u^2 + \frac{1}{4}} \qquad (5.8)$$

Example 1: Black-Scholes

$$\text{Im}\left[\phi_T(u - i/2)\right] = \text{Im}\left[e^{-\frac{1}{2}\left(u^2 + 1/4\right)\sigma^2 T}\right] = 0$$

Then, in the Black-Scholes case,

$$\left.\frac{\partial \sigma_{BS}(k, T)}{\partial k}\right|_{k=0} = 0 \quad \forall T > 0$$

Example 2: Merton's Jump Diffusion Model (JD) Write

$$\phi_T(u) = e^{-\frac{1}{2}u(u+i)\sigma^2 T} e^{\psi(u)T}$$

with $\psi(u) = -\lambda i u \left(e^{\alpha + \delta^2/2} - 1\right) + \lambda \left(e^{iu\alpha - u^2\delta^2/2} - 1\right)$
Then

$$\text{Im}\left[\phi_T(u - i/2)\right] = e^{-\frac{1}{2}\left(u^2 + \frac{1}{4}\right)\sigma^2 T} \text{Im}\left[e^{\psi(u - i/2)T}\right]$$

How Jumps Impact the Volatility Skew

By substituting the jump diffusion characteristic function (5.5) into our expressions (5.7) and (5.8) for the implied volatility and ATM volatility skew respectively, we can investigate the impact of jumps on the volatility surface for various numerical choices of the parameters.

Skew Behavior under Jump Diffusion as T → 0 Consider the value of an option under jump diffusion with a short time ΔT to expiration. Because the time to expiration is very short, the probability of having more than one jump is negligible. Because the jump is independent of the diffusion, the value of the option is just a superposition of the value conditional on the jump and the value conditional on no jump. Without loss of generality, suppose the stock price jumps down from S to JS when the jump occurs. Then

$$C_J(S, K, \Delta T) \approx (1 - \lambda \Delta T) \, C_{BS}(Se^{\mu_J \Delta T}, K, \Delta T) + \lambda \Delta T \, C(JS, K, \Delta T)$$

$$= C_{BS}(Se^{\mu_J \Delta T}, K, \Delta T) + O(\Delta T) \tag{5.9}$$

where J is the size of the jump, $C_J(.)$ represents the value of the option under jump diffusion and $\mu_J = -\lambda(e^{\alpha + \delta^2/2} - 1)$ is the adjustment to the risk-neutral drift for jumps. Here, we neglected the second term in equation (5.9) by assuming that the mean jump is downward and the probability of the option being in-the-money is negligibly small after the jump.

We want to compute the at-the-money variance skew

$$\left. \frac{\partial \sigma_{BS}^2}{\partial k} \right|_{k=0}$$

To do this note that

$$\frac{\partial C_J}{\partial k} = \frac{\partial C_{BS}}{\partial k} + \frac{\partial C_{BS}}{\partial \sigma_{BS}} \frac{\partial \sigma_{BS}}{\partial k}$$

so

$$\left. \frac{\partial \sigma_{BS}}{\partial k} \right|_{k=0} = \left[\frac{\partial C_J}{\partial k} - \frac{\partial C_{BS}}{\partial k} \right] \left(\frac{\partial C_{BS}}{\sigma_{BS}} \right)^{-1} \Bigg|_{k=0}$$

Now, for an at-the-money option,

$$\left. \frac{\partial C_{BS}}{\sigma_{BS}} \right|_{k=0} \approx \frac{S}{\sqrt{2\pi}} \sqrt{\Delta T}$$

and from equation (5.9)

$$\frac{1}{S} \left[\frac{\partial C_J}{\partial k} - \frac{\partial C_{BS}}{\partial k} \right] \Bigg|_{k=0} \approx -N \left(+\frac{\mu_J \Delta T}{\sigma \sqrt{\Delta T}} - \frac{1}{2} \sigma \sqrt{\Delta T} \right) + N \left(-\frac{1}{2} \sigma \sqrt{\Delta T} \right)$$

$$\approx -\frac{1}{\sqrt{2\pi}} \frac{\mu_J}{\sigma} \sqrt{\Delta T}$$

Then, for small ΔT,

$$\left. \frac{\partial \sigma_{BS}^2}{\partial k} \right|_{k=0} \approx -2 \mu_J \tag{5.10}$$

We see that in a jump diffusion model, if the mean jump size is sufficiently large relative to its standard deviation, the at-the-money variance skew is given directly by twice the jump compensator μ_J.

To see how well these approximate computations explain Figures 5.2 and 5.3, the characteristic time T^* and the time zero skew ψ_0 for each choice of parameters are presented in Table 5.3.

TABLE 5.2   Parameters used to generate Figures 5.2 and 5.3.

	σ	λ	α	δ
Solid	0.2	0.5	−0.15	0.05
Dashed	0.2	1.0	−0.07	0.00
Long-dashed	0.2	1.0	−0.07	0.05

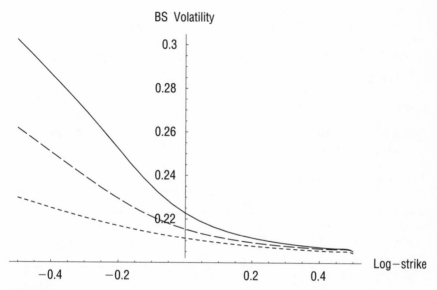

FIGURE 5.2   The 3-month volatility smile for various choices of jump diffusion parameters.

The Decay of Skew Due to Jumps   We can see from Figure 5.3 that the volatility skew decays very rapidly in a jump diffusion model beyond a certain time to expiration. To estimate this characteristic time, we note that prices of European options depend only on the final distribution of stock prices and if the jump size is of the order of only one standard deviation $\sigma \sqrt{T}$, a single jump has little impact on the shape of this distribution. From the discussion in the previous section, we know that the $T \to 0$ skew is given by the jump compensator μ_J. We can generate a given μ_J either with frequent small jumps or with infrequent big jumps. If there are many small jumps, returns will be hard to distinguish from normal over a reasonable time interval. On the other hand, if there are infrequent big jumps and time to expiration is sufficiently short, below some characteristic time T^* say,

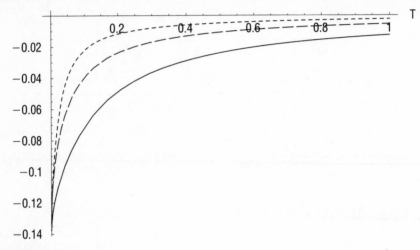

FIGURE 5.3   The term structure of ATM variance skew for various choices of jump diffusion parameters.

TABLE 5.3   Interpreting Figures 5.2 and 5.3.

	σ	λ	α	δ	T^*	ψ_0
Solid	0.2	0.5	−0.15	0.05	0.69	−0.133
Dashed	0.2	1.0	−0.07	0.00	0.34	−0.135
Long-dashed	0.2	1.0	−0.07	0.05	0.33	−0.133

we should be able to detect the presence of the jump in the final return distribution. We compute T^* by equating

$$-\left(e^{\alpha+\delta^2/2} - 1\right) \approx \sigma\sqrt{T^*}$$

To see this explicitly, Figure 5.4 shows the terminal return distributions for various expirations corresponding to the solid-line parameters from Table 5.2:

$$\sigma = 0.2; \ \lambda = 0.5; \ \alpha = -0.15; \ \delta = 0.05.$$

We see that as time to expiration T increases, the return distribution looks more and more normal so that at the characteristic time T^*, it's hard to tell that there is a jump.

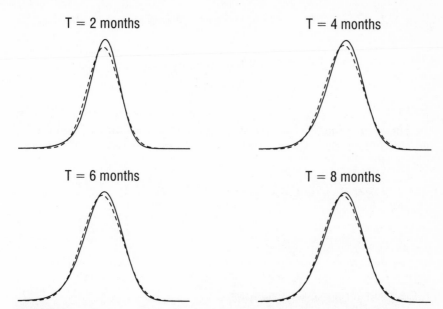

FIGURE 5.4 As time to expiration increases, the return distribution looks more and more normal. The solid line is the jump diffusion pdf and for comparison, the dashed line is the normal density with the same mean and standard deviation. With the parameters used to generate these plots, the characteristic time $T^* = 0.67$.

Summarizing the results, we note that the jump compensator (or expected move in the stock price due to jumps) drives the skew in the short-expiration limit while the decay of ATM skew is driven by the expected jump size.

STOCHASTIC VOLATILITY PLUS JUMPS

Stochastic Volatility Plus Jumps in the Underlying Only (SVJ)

Because jumps generate a steep short-dated skew that dies quickly with time to expiration and stochastic volatility models don't generate enough skew for very short expirations but more or less fit for longer expirations (see Chapter 3), it is natural to try to combine stock price jumps and stochastic volatility in one model.

Suppose we add a simple Merton-style lognormally distributed jump process to the Heston process so that

$$dS = \mu S\,dt + \sqrt{v}\,S\,dZ_1 + \left(e^{\alpha+\delta\epsilon} - 1\right)S\,dq$$
$$dv = -\lambda(v - \bar{v})\,dt + \eta\,\sqrt{v}\,dZ_2$$

with $\langle dZ_1 \, dZ_2 \rangle = \rho \, dt$, $\epsilon \sim N(0, 1)$ and as in the jump diffusion case, the Poisson process

$$dq = \begin{cases} 0 & \text{with probability } 1 - \lambda_J \, dt \\ 1 & \text{with probability } \lambda_J \, dt \end{cases}$$

where λ_J is the jump intensity (or hazard rate). By substitution into the valuation equation, it is easy to see that the characteristic function for this process is just the product of Heston and jump characteristic functions. Specifically,

$$\phi_T(u) = e^{C(u,T)\,\bar{v} + D(u,T)\,v} \, e^{\psi(u)T}$$

with $\psi(u) = -\lambda_J i u \left(e^{\alpha + \delta^2/2} - 1 \right) + \lambda_J \left(e^{iu\alpha - u^2\delta^2/2} - 1 \right)$ and $C(u, T)$, $D(u, T)$ are as before.

Again, we may substitute this functional form into equations (5.7) and (5.8) to get the implied volatilities and at-the-money volatility skew respectively for any given expiration.

Figure 5.5 plots the at-the-money variance skew corresponding to the Bakshi-Cao-Chen SVJ model fit together with the sum of the Heston and jump diffusion at-the-money variance skews with the same parameters (see Table 5.4). We see that (at least with this choice of parameters), not only does the characteristic function factorize but the at-the-money variance skew is almost additive. One practical consequence of this is that the Heston parameters can be fitted fairly robustly using longer dated options and then jump parameters can be found to generate the required extra skew for short-dated options. Figure 5.6 plots the at-the-money variance skew corresponding to the SVJ model vs the Heston model skew for short-dated options, highlighting the small difference.

However in the SVJ model, after the stock price has jumped, the volatility will stay unchanged because the jump process is uncorrelated with the volatility process. This is inconsistent with both intuition and empirically observed properties of the time series of asset returns; in practice, after a large move in the underlying, implied volatilities always increase substantially (i.e., they jump).

Some Empirical Fits to the SPX Volatility Surface

There are only four parameters in the jump diffusion model: the volatility σ, λ_J, α and δ so it's not in principle difficult to perform a fit to option price data. The SVJ model obviously fits the data better because it has more parameters and it's not technically that much harder to perform the fit.

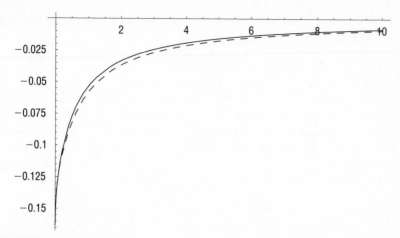

FIGURE 5.5 The solid line is a graph of the at-the-money variance skew in the SVJ model with BCC parameters vs. time to expiration. The dashed line represents the sum of at-the-money Heston and jump diffusion skews with the same parameters.

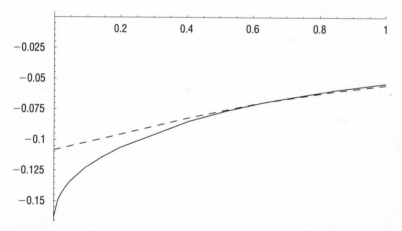

FIGURE 5.6 The solid line is a graph of the at-the-money variance skew in the SVJ model with BCC parameters versus time to expiration. The dashed line represents the at-the-money Heston skew with the same parameters.

Various authors, for example, Andersen and Andreasen (2000) and Duffie, Pan, and Singleton (2000), have fitted JD and SVJ models to SPX data. Their results are summarized in Table 5.4.

Note first that these estimates all relate to different dates so in principle, we can't expect the volatility surfaces they generate to be the same shape.

Nevertheless, the shape of the SPX volatility surface doesn't really change much over time so it does make some sense to compare them.

A Note on the AA Estimate   The one estimate that sticks out is obviously the AA JD fit with a huge expected jump size of -0.8898. At first sight, it might seem disconcerting that imputing jump parameters from implied volatility surfaces could give rise to such wildly different parameter estimates. On closer inspection of the Andersen and Andreasen (2000) paper however, the AA jump size estimate turns out to have been driven by requiring the fit to match the 10-year volatility skew and as pointed out earlier, for the characteristic time T^* to be of the order of 10 years, we need a huge jump size. However, the overall AA fit of JD to the implied volatility surface is very poor; JD is completely misspecified and we can confidently reject JD with AA parameters.

Stochastic Volatility with Simultaneous Jumps in Stock Price and Volatility (SVJJ)

As we noted earlier in our discussion of the SVJ model, it is unrealistic to suppose that the instantaneous volatility wouldn't jump if the stock price were to jump. Conversely, adding a simultaneous upward jump in volatility to jumps in the stock price allows us to maintain the clustering property of stochastic volatility models: Recall that "large moves follow large moves and small moves follow small moves."

In Matytsin (1999) and Matytsin (2000), Andrew Matytsin describes a model that is effectively SVJ with a jump in volatility: jumps in the stock price are accompanied by a jump $v \mapsto v + \gamma_v$ in the instantaneous volatility. In that case, the characteristic function is

$$\phi_T(u) = \exp\left\{ \hat{C}(u, T)\,\bar{v} + \hat{D}(u, T)\,v \right\} \tag{5.11}$$

with $C(u, T)$ and $D(u, T)$ given by

$$\hat{C}(u, T) = C(u, T) + \lambda_J\,T\left[e^{iu\alpha - u^2\delta^2/2} I(u, T) - 1 - iu\left(e^{\alpha + \delta^2/2} - 1 \right) \right]$$

$$\hat{D}(u, T) = D(u, T)$$

where

$$I(u, T) = \frac{1}{T}\int_0^T e^{\gamma_v D(u,t)}\,dt$$

$$= -\frac{1}{T}\frac{2\gamma_v}{p_+ p_-}\int_0^{-\gamma_v D(u,T)} \frac{e^{-z}\,dz}{(1 + z/p_+)(1 + z/p_-)}$$

TABLE 5.4 Various fits of jump diffusion style models to SPX data. JD means *Jump Diffusion* and SVJ means *Stochastic Volatility plus Jumps*.

Author(s)	Model	λ	η	ρ	$\bar{v}$	λ_J	α	δ
AA	JD	NA	NA	NA	0.032	0.089	−0.8898	0.4505
BCC	SVJ	2.03	0.38	−0.57	0.04	0.59	−0.05	0.07
M	SVJ	1.0	0.8	−0.7	0.04	0.5	−0.15	0
DPS	SVJ	3.99	0.27	−0.79	0.014	0.11	−0.12	0.15
JG	SVJ	0.54	0.30	−0.70	0.044	0.13	−0.12	0.10

Author(s)	Reference	Data from
AA	Andersen and Andreasen (2000)	April 1999
BCC	Bakshi, Cao, and Chen (1997)	June 1988 to May 1991
M	Matytsin (1999)	1999
DPS	Duffie, Pan, and Singleton (2000)	November 1993
JG	This chapter	September 2005

and

$$p_\pm = \frac{\gamma_v}{\eta^2}(\beta - \rho\eta u i \pm d)$$

In the limit $\gamma_v \to 0$, we have $I(u, T) \to 1$ and by inspection, we retrieve the SVJ model. Also, in the limit $T \to 0$, $I(u, T) \to 1$ and in that limit, the SVJJ characteristic function is identical to the SVJ characteristic function. Alternatively, following our earlier heuristic argument, the short-dated volatility skew is a function of the jump compensator only and this compensator is identical in the SVJ and SVJJ cases. Intuitively, when the stock price jumps, the volatility jumps but this has no effect in the $T \to 0$ limit because by assumption, an at-the-money option is always out-of-the-money after the jump and its time value is zero no matter what the volatility is.

On the other hand, in the $T \to \infty$ limit, the skew should increase because the effective volatility of volatility increases due to (random) jumps in volatility.

By substituting the SVJJ characteristic function (5.11) into equation (5.8) for the implied volatility skew with the BCC parameters plus a variance jump of $\gamma_v = 0.1$, we obtain the graphs shown in Figures 5.7 and 5.8. We note that the term structure of volatility skew is in accordance with our intuition. In particular, adding a jump in volatility doesn't help explain extreme short-dated volatility skews. However relative to stochastic

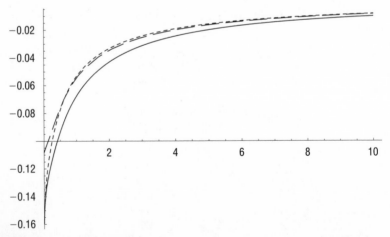

FIGURE 5.7 The solid line is a graph of the at-the-money variance skew in the SVJJ model with BCC parameters versus time to expiration. The short-dashed and long-dashed lines are SVJ and Heston skew graphs respectively with the same parameters.

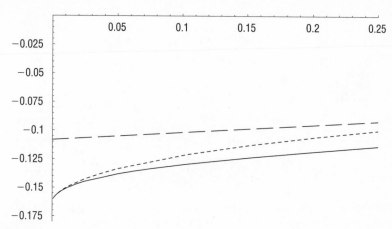

FIGURE 5.8   This graph is a short-expiration detailed view of the graph shown in Figure 5.7.

volatility and SVJ models, it does reduce the volatility of volatility required to fit longer-dated volatility skews even if that comes at the expense of a seemingly even more unreasonable estimate for the average stock price jump.

SVJ Fit to the September 15, 2005, SPX Option Data

In Table 5.5, we list Heston parameters obtained from a fit to the September 15, 2005, SPX volatility surface graphed in Figure 3.2.

As in Chapter 3, a good way to see how well the SVJ model fits the empirical implied volatility surface overall is to compare the two volatility surfaces graphically. We see from Figure 5.9 that in contrast to the Heston

TABLE 5.5   SVJ fit to the SPX surface as of the close on September 15, 2005.

v	0.0158
$\bar{v}$	0.0439
η	0.3038
ρ	−0.6974
λ	0.5394
λ_J	0.1308
δ	0.0967
α	−0.1151

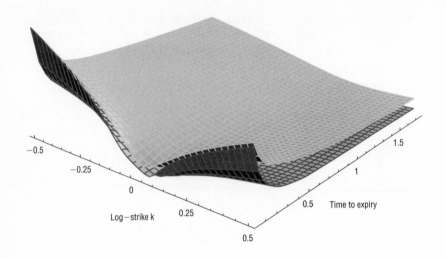

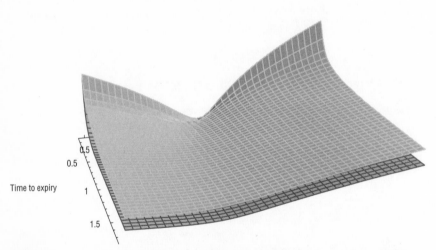

FIGURE 5.9 Comparison of the empirical SPX implied volatility surface with the SVJ fit as of September 15, 2005. From the two views presented here, we can see that in contrast to the Heston case, the major features of the empirical surface are replicated by the SVJ model. The paler upper surface is the empirical SPX volatility surface and the darker lower one the SVJ fit. The SVJ fit surface has again been shifted down by five volatility points for ease of visual comparison.

case graphed in Figure 3.6, the SVJ model succeeds in generating a volatility surface that has the main features of the empirical surface although the fit is not perfect. Again, for longer expirations, the fit is pretty good.

Why the SVJ Model Wins

We have already remarked that SVJ fits the observed implied volatility surface reasonably well in contrast to the Heston model. The reader might wonder whether making dynamics more reasonable by including jumps in volatility as in the SVJJ model might generate surfaces that fit even better. Sadly, we can see from Figures 5.7 and 5.8 that not only does the SVJJ model have more parameters than the SVJ model, but it's harder to fit to observed option prices. The SVJ model thus emerges as a clear winner in the comparison between Heston, SVJ and SVJJ models.

CHAPTER **6**

Modeling Default Risk

I t's clear from Chapter 5 that jumps are required to explain the shape of the implied volatility surface. In the single-stock case, there is a much more direct and obvious explanation for the volatility skew: default risk. We shall see that if the credit spread—and so default risk—is high, implied volatility skews can be extreme.

MERTON'S MODEL OF DEFAULT

As we have come to expect, Wilmott (2000) gives an excellent introduction to the modeling of default risk. There are two broad types of default risk model used by practitioners: so-called *structural* models and so-called *reduced form* models. I found the following useful description by Jabairu Stork on Wilmott.com:

> A structural model *(of firm default) postulates that default occurs when some economic variable (like firm value) crosses some barrier (like debt value), typically using a contingent claims model to support this assertion and to find the probability of default. Both H-W and Creditgrades* are models of this form.*
>
> A reduced form *model models default as a random occurrence—there is no observable or latent variable which triggers the default event, it just happens. The Duffie and Singleton (1999) model is a reduced form model. These models are easy to calibrate, but because they lack any ability to explain why default happens, I think they make most people nervous. Basically, you estimate an intensity for the arrival of default (possibly as a function of time, possibly as a stochastic process, possibly as a function of other things.)*

---

*See Finkelstein (2002) and Lardy (2002).

74

The model introduced in Merton (1974) is the simplest possible example of a reduced form model. It supposes that there some probability $\lambda(t)$ per unit time of the stock price jumping to zero (the *hazard rate*), whereupon default occurs. Jumps are independent of the stock price process. Then, contingent claims must satisfy the jump diffusion valuation equation (5.3) with $\mathbb{E}[J] = 0$. It is particulary straightforward to value a call option because for a call, $V(SJ, t) = 0$. Substitution into equation (5.3) gives

$$\frac{\partial V}{\partial t} + \frac{1}{2}\sigma^2 S^2 \frac{\partial^2 V}{\partial S^2} + rS\frac{\partial V}{\partial S} - rV - \lambda(t)\left\{V - S\frac{\partial V}{\partial S}\right\} = 0 \qquad (6.1)$$

We immediately recognize equation (6.1) as the Black-Scholes equation with a shifted interest rate $r + \lambda$. Its solution is of course the Black-Scholes formula with this shifted rate.

The meaning of this shifted rate is particularly clear if we assume no recovery (in the case of default) on the issuer's bonds so that $B(JS, t) = 0$. Then, the risky bond price $B(t, T)$ must also satisfy equation (6.1) with the solution

$$B(t, T) = e^{-\int_t^T (r(s) + \lambda(s))ds}$$

We identify the shifted rate $r + \lambda$ with the yield (risk-free rate plus credit spread) of a risky bond. The situation is a little more complicated (but not too much more) if we allow some recovery R on default.

Intuition

It may at first seem surprising that the Black-Scholes formula could be a solution of an equation that has a jump to zero (the so-called *jump to ruin*) in it. There is an economic reason for this, however.

Recall that the derivation of the Black-Scholes formula involves the construction of a replicating portfolio for a call option involving just stock and risk-free bonds. Suppose instead, we were to construct this portfolio using stock and risky bonds. So long as there is no jump to ruin, the derivation goes through as before and the portfolio is self-financing. If there is a jump to ruin, assuming no recovery on the bond, both the bond and the stock jump to zero—the portfolio is still self-financing!

What would happen if we were to hedge a short call option position using stock and *risk-free* bonds following the standard Black-Scholes hedging recipe (as most practitioners actually do)? We would be long stock and short risk-free bonds and, in the case of default, the call would end up worthless, the stock would be worthless, and we would get full recovery on our risk-free bonds. In other words, on default, we would have a windfall gain. On the other hand, relative to hedging with risky bonds, we would forego the higher carry (or yield).

Implications for the Volatility Skew

All issuers of stock have some probability of defaulting. There is a very active credit derivative market that prices default-risk (see Default-Risk.com for background). Black-Scholes implied volatilities are computed by inserting the risk-free rate into the Black-Scholes formula. However, as we just showed, in Merton's model, call option prices are correctly obtained by substituting the risky rate into the Black-Scholes formula. This induces a skew that can become extremely steep for short-dated options on stocks whose issuers have high credit spreads.

In Figure 6.1, we graph the implied volatility for various issuer credit spreads assuming that options are correctly priced using the Merton model. We see that the downside skew that the model generates can be extreme.

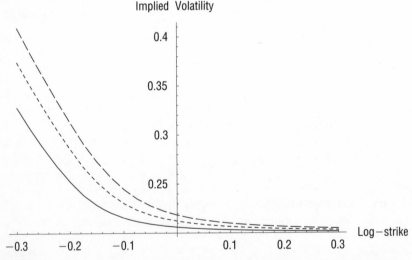

FIGURE 6.1 Three-month implied volatilities from the Merton model assuming a stock volatility of 20% and credit spreads of 100 bp (solid), 200 bp (dashed) and 300 bp (long-dashed).

CAPITAL STRUCTURE ARBITRAGE

Capital structure arbitrage is the term used to describe the fashion for arbitraging equity claims against fixed income and convertible claims. At its most sophisticated, practitioners build elaborate models of the capital structure of a company to determine the relative values of the various claims—in particular, stock, bonds, and convertible bonds. At its simplest, the trader looks to see if equity puts are cheaper than credit derivatives and if so buys the one and sells the other. To understand this, we review put-call parity.

Put-Call Parity

We saw previously that in the Merton model the value of an equity call option is given by the Black-Scholes formula for a call with the risk-free rate replaced by the risky rate. What about put options? To make the previous arguments work, the put option would need to be worthless after the jump to ruin occurs. That would be the case if the put in question were to be written by the issuer of the stock. In that case, when default occurs, assuming zero recovery, the put options would also be worth nothing. So the Black-Scholes formula for a put with the risk-free rate replaced by the risky rate does value put options written by the issuer.

What about put options written by some default-free counterparty (for example, an exchange)? When default occurs, this put option should be worth the strike price. We already know how to value a call written by a default-free counterparty; by definition, the issuer of a stock cannot default on a call on his or her own stock, so the value of a call written by the issuer of the stock equals the value of a call written by a default-free counterparty. We obtain the value of a put by put-call parity: using risk-free bonds in the case of the default-free counterparty and risky bonds in the case of the risky counterparty.

Denoting the value of a risk-free put, call and bond by P_0, C_0, and B_0 and the value of risky claims on the issuer (I) of the stock by P_I, C_I, and B_I, we obtain

$$P_0 = C_0 + KB_0 - S \text{ (from put-call parity with risk-free bonds)}$$

$$= C_I + KB_0 - S \text{ (risk-free and issuer-written calls have the same value)}$$

$$= P_I + S - KB_I + KB_0 - S \text{ (from put-call parity with risky bonds)}$$

$$= P_I + K(B_0 - B_I)$$

As we would expect, the risk-free put is worth more than the risky put. The excess value is equal to the difference in risky and risk-free bond prices (times the strike price). With maturity-independent rates and credit spreads for clarity and setting $t = 0$, we obtain

$$B_0 - B_I = e^{-rT}\left(1 - e^{-\lambda T}\right)$$

which is just the discounted probability of default in the Merton model. In words, the extra value is the strike price times the (pseudo-) probability that default occurs. This payoff is also more or less exactly the payoff of a default put in the credit derivatives market.

The Arbitrage

Referring back to Figure 6.1, we see that the downside implied volatility skew can be extreme for stocks whose issuers have high credit spreads. Equity option market makers (until recently at least) made do with heuristic rules to determine whether a skew looked reasonable or not; implied volatility skews of the magnitude shown in Figure 6.1 seemed just too extreme to be considered reasonable. Taking advantage of the market maker's lack of understanding, the trader buys an equity option on the exchange at a "very high" (but, of course, insufficiently high) implied volatility and sells a default put on the same stock in the credit derivatives market locking in a risk-free return.

This actually happened and hedge funds were able to lock in risk-free gains for a period of time. During this period, market makers saw what were to them extremely steep volatility skews get even steeper and they lost money.

Ultimately, skews became so steep that the hedge funds made money risk-free the other way round—through put spreads. A popular trade for a hedge fund was to buy one at-the-money put and sell two puts struck at half the current stock price. As we can see from Figure 6.2, this strategy has only positive payoffs so if this can be traded flat or for a net credit, it is a pure arbitrage.

The life of a market maker is not a happy one—it seems that graduate degree level understanding is required to avoid getting arbitraged!

We see that there is a lower bound to the price of a put given by the credit default swap market and an upper bound given by spread arbitrage. To make this more concrete, consider the upper and lower bounds for a 0.5 strike one-year option with credit spreads of 100 bp, 200 bp and 300 bp displayed in Table 6.1.

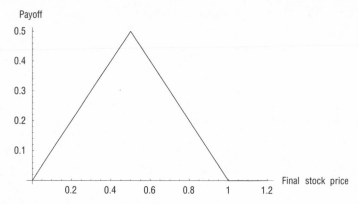

FIGURE 6.2   Payoff of the 1 × 2 put spread combination: buy one put with strike 1.0 and sell two puts with strike 0.5.

TABLE 6.1   Upper and lower arbitrage bounds for one-year 0.5 strike options for various credit spreads (at-the-money volatility is 20%).

Credit Spread (bp)	Lower Bound	Upper Bound
250	0.0123	0.0398
500	0.0244	0.0398
750	0.0361	0.0398

Assuming 20% at-the-money volatility, the upper bound is computed as half the value of an at-the-money option which is 0.0398 in each case. On the other hand, the lower bounds are just the present value of the strike price* times the probability of default. We see that the lower bound increases steadily towards the upper bound as the credit spread increases *for fixed at-the-money implied volatility*. It's easy to see how a market maker could have exceeded the upper bound given the steady increase in skews.

LOCAL AND IMPLIED VOLATILITY IN THE JUMP-TO-RUIN MODEL

As noted already, the value of a call option is given by the Black-Scholes formula with the interest rate shifted by the hazard rate.

---

*We are still assuming zero rates so the PV factor is always one.

We recall formula (1.6) for local volatility from Chapter 1:

$$\sigma_{loc}^2(K,T,S) = \frac{\frac{\partial C}{\partial T}}{\frac{1}{2}K^2 \frac{\partial^2 C}{\partial K^2}} \tag{6.2}$$

Because the Black-Scholes formula C for a call option is linearly homogenous in the stock price S and the strike price K, we have the relation

$$C = S\frac{\partial C}{\partial S} + K\frac{\partial C}{\partial K}$$

It follows that

$$K^2 \frac{\partial^2 C}{\partial K^2} = S^2 \frac{\partial^2 C}{\partial S^2}$$

Also, in the jump-to-ruin case with zero interest rates and dividends, we have

$$\frac{\partial C}{\partial T} = \frac{1}{2}\sigma^2 S^2 \frac{\partial^2 C}{\partial S^2} + \lambda S\frac{\partial C}{\partial S} - \lambda C$$

where σ is the volatility (diffusion coefficient) and λ is the hazard rate. Rewriting this in terms of derivatives with respect to K gives

$$\frac{\partial C}{\partial T} = \frac{1}{2}\sigma^2 K^2 \frac{\partial^2 C}{\partial K^2} - \lambda K\frac{\partial C}{\partial K}$$

Substituting into equation (6.2) gives

$$\sigma_{loc}^2(K,T,S) = \sigma^2 - \lambda\,\frac{K\frac{\partial C}{\partial K}}{\frac{1}{2}K^2 \frac{\partial^2 C}{\partial K^2}}$$

$$= \sigma^2 + 2\lambda\sigma\sqrt{T}\,\frac{N(d_2)}{N'(d_2)}$$

with

$$d_2 = \frac{\log S/K + \lambda T}{\sigma\sqrt{T}} - \frac{\sigma\sqrt{T}}{2}$$

For very low strikes $K/S \ll 1$, we have $d_2 \gg 0$ and

$$N(d_2) \approx 1$$

$$N'(d_2) = \frac{1}{\sqrt{2\pi}} \, e^{-d_2^2/2}$$

Then, for very low strikes,

$$\sigma_{loc}^2(K, T, S) \approx \sigma^2 + 2\lambda\sigma\sqrt{T}\sqrt{2\pi}\, e^{+d_2^2/2}$$

Figure 6.3 shows a typical jump-to-ruin local variance surface. From Chapter 3, we know that implied variance (volatility squared) is a gamma-weighted average of local variances. It follows that implied volatility in the jump-to-ruin model increases very fast as the strike decreases from at-the-money and tends to the constant σ for high strikes—exactly consistent with Figure 6.1 and quite different from the stochastic volatility case.

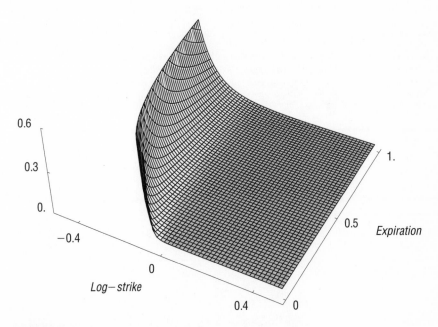

FIGURE 6.3 Local variance plot with $\lambda = 0.05$ and $\sigma = 0.2$.

THE EFFECT OF DEFAULT RISK ON OPTION PRICES

To make the foregoing a little more concrete, consider the implied volatilities of January-05 options on GT (Goodyear Tire and Rubber) as of October 20, 2004.

We noted earlier that the price of a European call option in the Merton jump-to-ruin model is given by the Black-Scholes formula with a shifted interest rate. Our experiment is to find the shifted rate and constant volatility that generate prices closest to the European option prices* computed using these implied volatilities (i.e., the best fit parameters of the Merton model).

We find the best fit parameters:

$$\lambda = 0.01934$$

$$\sigma = 0.3946$$

With these parameters, we may compute call option prices and compute the standard (risk-free) Black-Scholes implied volatilities. The results are shown in Table 6.2.

In fact, because GT credit spreads are very high, the Merton model fits the left wing of the volatility skew very well as shown in Figure 6.4.

TABLE 6.2   Implied volatilities for January 2005 options on GT as of October 20, 2004 (GT was trading at 9.40). Merton vols are volatilities generated from the Merton model with fitted parameters.

Strike	Bid Vol.	Ask Vol.	Merton Vol.
2.50		147.2%	145.2%
5.00	73.6%	88.3%	85.8%
7.50	48.3%	58.2%	51.2%
10.00	38.1%	45.0%	43.1%
12.50	41.2%	48.1%	41.5%
15.00	51.2%	54.3%	40.9%
17.50	64.5%	66.5%	40.6%
20.00		77.3%	40.0%
25.00		94.7%	40.0%
30.00		108.3%	40.0%

---

*Note that traded options are American. We are making the reasonable assumption here that American implied volatilities are close to European implied volatilities.

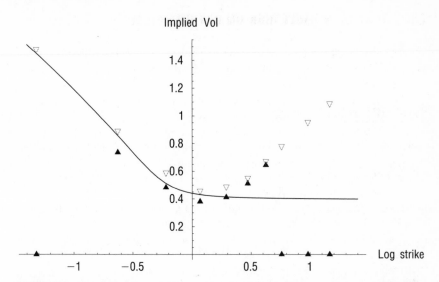

FIGURE 6.4 The triangles represent bid and offer volatilities and the solid line is the Merton model fit.

However, the Merton model produces a skew that is a little too steep for low strikes and as predicted generates no right wing (high strike structure) at all and that's just not consistent with the data. As we are by now well aware from our study of stochastic volatility, the positively sloped right wing in the empirically observed volatility surface reflects uncertainty in the future level of volatility; the flat right wing in the Merton model reflects its deterministic volatility assumption.

Finally, we might ask whether or not the fitted parameters are realistic. The volatility estimate $\sigma = 39.46\%$ is clearly realistic from inspection of the implied volatilities. To see that the hazard rate estimate of $\lambda = 0.01934$ is also realistic, we note that the fair price of a zero coupon bond of GT (assuming zero rates) should be given by

$$P_t = e^{-\lambda t} R + (1 - e^{-\lambda t})$$

where R is the recovery rate. With Bloomberg's standard assumed recovery rate of 0.4, the credit spread of this bond would be found by solving

$$P_t = e^{-ct} = e^{-\lambda t} R + (1 - e^{-\lambda t})$$

With the above choices of λ and R, we obtain

$$c = 4.58\%$$

This compares with the 5-year credit default swap (CDS) rate of over 5% for GT; the derived credit spread is almost certainly too high for 3-month paper. However, the main point remains: most of the volatility skew for stocks with high credit spreads can be ascribed to default risk.

THE CREDITGRADES MODEL

If Merton's jump-to-ruin model is the prototypical reduced form model, then the prototypical structural model is the one due to Black and Scholes (1973) and Merton (1974) that models equity as a call option on the value of a company. The value of the company V is assumed to diffuse with no jumps. Debt is then equivalent to a call writer's position of long V and short the call on V. There is then a very natural connection between the stock price and stock volatility; as the stock price declines, the company gets more leveraged and stock volatility increases, exactly as observed empirically. Obviously, this generates an implied volatility skew too.

The one big practical problem with this simple model is that there is no way to generate significant short-dated credit spreads; default occurs when the value of the company hits a certain level below the current value and for short times, there is insufficient time for the V process to diffuse to the barrier. Finkelstein (2002) and Lardy (2002) resolve this by making the level of the default barrier uncertain. This extra feature is even intuitive: Who would claim to know exactly what level V would have to reach for default to occur? For example American Airlines (AMR) currently has negative book value but has an enterprise value of over $13 billion.

Model Setup

V is assumed to evolve as a driftless geometric Brownian motion, so

$$\frac{dV_t}{V_t} = \sigma \, dW$$

where σ is the volatility of firm value V.

The level of V at which the company defaults is given by $L D$ where D is today's value of its debt (per share) and L is the recovery rate. As discussed above, it is further assumed that the recovery rate L is a lognormally distributed random variable with mean $\overline{L}$ and standard deviation λ so that

$$L D = \overline{L} D \, e^{\lambda Z - \lambda^2/2}$$

where $Z \sim N(0, 1)$. The random variable Z is assumed to be independent of W_t.

Survival Probability

Define

$$X_t := \sigma\, W_t - \lambda\, Z - \frac{\sigma^2 t}{2} - \frac{\lambda^2}{2}$$

Then X_t is normally distributed with

$$\mathbb{E}\,[X_t] = -\frac{\sigma^2}{2}\left(t + \frac{\lambda^2}{\sigma^2}\right)$$

$$\text{Var}\,[X_t] = \sigma^2\left(t + \frac{\lambda^2}{\sigma^2}\right)$$

This leads us to approximate X with a Brownian motion $\hat{X}$ with drift $-\sigma^2/2$ and variance σ^2 that starts at 0 at the time $-\Delta t := -\lambda^2/\sigma^2$ with $\hat{X}_{-\Delta t} = 0$. Obviously X isn't really a Brownian motion with drift but its moments agree with those of $\hat{X}$ for $t \geq 0$.

Default occurs when

$$V = V_0\, e^{\sigma\, W_t - \sigma^2 t/2} = L\,D = \overline{L}\,D\, e^{\lambda Z - \lambda^2/2}$$

or equivalently when

$$X_t = \log\left(\frac{\overline{L}\,D}{V_0}\right) - \lambda^2$$

Since $\hat{X}$ is a Brownian motion with drift, the probability of survival (or the probability of not hitting the default barrier) is given by the Black-Scholes-like formula

$$P_t = N\left(-\frac{A_t}{2} + \frac{\log d}{A_t}\right) - d\,N\left(-\frac{A_t}{2} - \frac{\log d}{A_t}\right)$$

with

$$d = \frac{V_0\, e^{\lambda^2}}{\overline{L}\,D};\ A_t^2 = \sigma^2 t + \lambda^2$$

Since P_t is the probability of survival up to time t, it may be estimated directly from the prices of risky instruments such as bonds and credit default swaps (CDS).

As an aside, we could avoid approximating X with $\hat{X}$ by computing the survival probability conditional on a given default barrier level L and integrating over the distribution of barrier levels. This gives rise to an expression for the survival probability that contains the cumulative bivariate density but is numerically little different in practice.

Equity Volatility

The stock price S is approximately related (neglecting the time value of the option) to the firm value V via

$$V \approx LD + S$$

Then

$$\sigma \sim \frac{\delta V}{V} \approx \frac{\delta S}{S + LD} = \frac{\delta S}{S} \frac{S}{S + LD} \sim \sigma_S \frac{S}{S + LD}$$

where σ_S is the stock volatility. We see that as the stock price rises, keeping σ fixed, the volatility σ_S of the stock declines. Conversely, as the stock price S approaches zero, the stock volatility increases as $1/S$.

Model Calibration

We end up with the following model in terms of market observables

$$P_t = N\left(-\frac{A_t}{2} + \frac{\log d}{A_t}\right) - d N\left(-\frac{A_t}{2} - \frac{\log d}{A_t}\right) \tag{6.3}$$

with

$$d = \frac{S_0 + \overline{L} D}{\overline{L} D} e^{\lambda^2}; \quad A_t^2 = \left(\sigma_S^* \frac{S^*}{S^* + \overline{L} D}\right)^2 t + \lambda^2$$

where S^* is some reference stock price and σ_S^* the stock volatility at that price.

In the technical document Finger (2002), $\overline{L}$ and λ are derived from historical recovery data and D is from balance sheet data. With sufficiently many bonds, we could also impute all of the parameters from the term structure of credit spreads (or equivalently, the term structure of the survival probability P_t). Getting $\overline{L}$, λ and D from company and industry data rather than from the term structure of credit spreads would theoretically enable us to identify rich and cheap claims.

From our perspective however, we content ourselves with the realization that once again, credit spreads are explicitly related to the volatility skew, only this time in the context of a more realistic model.

CHAPTER 7

Volatility Surface Asymptotics

From the discussion so far, the reader might wonder to what extent the results derived and the fits shown are tied to the precise form of the dynamics assumed. In this chapter, we investigate the shape of the volatility surface for very generic models of the stochastic volatility with jumps type. We see that, in fact, all such models generate volatility surfaces with a similar shape. In particular, we will see that it's practically impossible to deduce anything about the specific form of the volatility dynamics from a single observation of the volatility surface.

SHORT EXPIRATIONS

We start by rewriting our original general stochastic volatility SDEs (1.1) and (1.2) in terms of the log-moneyness $x := \log{(F/K)}$ and under the risk neutral measure, specializing to the case where α and β do not depend on S or t.

$$dx = -\frac{v}{2}dt + \sqrt{v}\,dZ_1$$
$$dv = \alpha\,(v)\,dt + \eta\sqrt{v}\beta\,(v)\,dZ_2 \qquad (7.1)$$

We may rewrite

$$dZ_2 = \rho dZ_1 + \varphi\,dZ_1^*$$

with $\varphi = \sqrt{1 - \rho^2}$ and $\langle dZ_1^*, dZ_1 \rangle = 0$. Eliminating $\sqrt{v}dZ_1$, we get

$$dv = \alpha\,(v, t)\,dt + \rho\eta\,\beta\,(v, t)\left\{dx + \frac{v}{2}dt\right\} + \varphi\eta\,\beta\,(v)\,\sqrt{v}\,dZ_1^*$$

Then,

$$\mathbb{E}[v + dv|dx] = v + \alpha\,(v)\,dt + \rho\eta\,\beta\,(v)\,\left\{dx + \frac{v}{2}dt\right\}$$

so for small times to expiration (relative to the variation of $\alpha(v)$ and $\beta(v)$), we have

$$v_{loc}(x,t) = \mathbb{E}\,[v_t\,|x_t = x]$$
$$\approx v_0 + \left[\alpha(v_0) + \rho\eta\frac{v_0}{2}\beta(v_0)\right]t + \rho\eta\beta(v_0)\,x \qquad (7.2)$$

The coefficient of x (the slope of the skew) here agrees with that derived by Lee (2001) using a perturbation expansion approach.

To extend the result to implied volatility, we need the following lemma:

Lemma The local volatility skew is twice as steep as the implied volatility skew for short times to expiration.

Proof From Chapter 3, we know that Black-Scholes implied total variance is the integral of local variance along the most probable path from the stock price on the valuation date to the strike price at expiration. This path is approximately a straight line (see Figure 7.1).

Also, from equation (7.2), we see that the slope of the local variance skew is a roughly constant $\beta(v_0)$ for short times. The BS implied variance skew, being the average of the local variance skews, is one half of the local variance skew. Formally,

$$\sigma_{BS}(K,T)^2 \approx \frac{1}{T}\int_0^T v_{loc}(\tilde{x}_t, t)dt$$
$$\approx \text{const.} + \frac{1}{T}\int_0^T \rho\eta\beta(v_0)\tilde{x}_t dt$$
$$\approx \text{const.} + \frac{1}{T}\int_0^T \rho\eta\beta(v_0)x_T\frac{t}{T}dt$$
$$= \text{const.} + \frac{1}{2}\rho\eta\beta(v_0)\,x_T$$

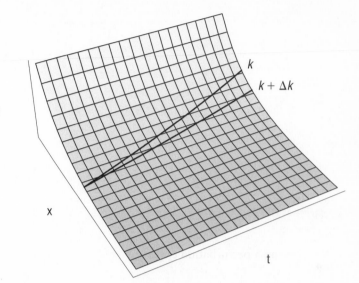

Local variance

FIGURE 7.1 For short expirations, the most probable path is approximately a straight line from spot on the valuation date to the strike at expiration. It follows that $\sigma_{BS}^2(k, T) \approx \left[v_{loc}(0,0) + v_{loc}(k, T) \right] /2$ and the implied variance skew is roughly one half of the local variance skew.

where $\tilde{x}$ represents the "most probable" path from the stock price at time zero to the strike price at expiration. □

We conclude that for short times to expiration, the BS implied variance skew is given by

$$\frac{\partial}{\partial x} \sigma_{BS}(x, t)^2 = \frac{\rho \eta}{2} \beta(v_0) \qquad (7.3)$$

Recall that in the Heston model, $\beta(v) = 1$ we see that equation (7.3) is consistent with the short-dated volatility skew behavior that we derived earlier in Chapter 7 for the Heston model.

THE MEDVEDEV-SCAILLET RESULT

It turns out that we can do much better than the heuristic argument of Chapter 5 to compute the contribution of jumps in the limit of small time to expiration. In a working paper, Medvedev and Scaillet (2004) develop a perturbation expansion for small times to expiration τ and fixed normalized log-strike z defined as

$$z := \frac{k}{\sigma_{BS}(k, \tau)\sqrt{\tau}}$$

First specializing their result to the case where the underlying process is a diffusion of the form

$$\frac{dS_t}{S_t} = \sigma_t \, dZ_1$$

$$d\sigma_t = a\left(\sigma_t\right) dt + b\left(\sigma_t\right) dZ_2 \qquad (7.4)$$

we find that the implied volatility I has the following short-term asymptotics (with $\sigma = \sigma_0$)

$$I(z, \tau, \sigma) = \sigma + I_1(z; \sigma)\sqrt{\tau} + I_2(z; \sigma)\tau + O(\tau\sqrt{\tau})$$

where I_1 and I_2 are functions of z and the instantaneous volatility $\sigma = \sqrt{v}$ only:

$$I_1(z; \sigma) = \frac{\rho\, b(\sigma)\, z}{2}$$

$$I_2(z; \sigma) = \frac{1}{6}\left\{ \frac{b(\sigma)^2\,(1 - \rho^2)}{\sigma} + \rho^2\, b(\sigma)\, \partial_\sigma b(\sigma) \right\} z^2$$

$$+ \frac{a(\sigma)}{2} + \frac{\rho\,\sigma\, b(\sigma)}{4} + \frac{1}{24}\frac{\rho^2\, b(\sigma)^2}{\sigma}$$

$$+ \frac{1}{12}\frac{b(\sigma)^2}{\sigma} - \frac{1}{6}\rho^2\, b(\sigma)\, \partial_\sigma b(\sigma) \qquad (7.5)$$

We note that the limit of implied volatility as the log-strike $k \to 0$ and the time to expiration $\tau \to 0$ is just the instantaneous volatility σ. So although critics of stochastic volatility models love to point out that instantaneous volatility is not observable and that this is a deficiency of such models, we see that this deficiency is not a major limitation in practice. In liquid option markets, the implied volatility surface is typically very smooth and we can extrapolate to the zero expiration, at-the-money strike limit with little uncertainty.

To compute the short-dated volatility skew, we substitute

$$z = \frac{k}{I(z, \tau; \sigma)\sqrt{\tau}}$$

into (7.5) and take the limit $\tau \to 0$ in order to obtain

$$\left. \frac{\partial I}{\partial k} \right|_{k=0} \to \frac{\rho\, b(\sigma)}{2\,\sigma} \qquad (7.6)$$

which proves our earlier result (7.3) derived using heuristic methods.

We note that the short-dated volatility skew is not explicitly time-dependent; it depends only on the form of the SDE for volatility.

In contrast, as we shall see, local volatility models imply short-dated skews that decay rapidly as time advances. So even if we find a stochastic volatility model and a local volatility model that price all European options identically today, forward-starting options (i.e., options whose strikes are to be set some time in the future) cannot possibly be priced identically by these two models. Both models fit the options market today, but the volatility surface dynamics implied by the two models are quite different.

Equations (7.3) and (7.6) suggest a wild generalization: perhaps all stochastic volatility models, whether analytically tractable or not, generate the same BS implied volatility skew up to a factor of $\beta(v)$, not just in the limit $\tau \to 0$ but for all $\tau \geq 0$. Later on, we will investigate the behavior of the volatility skew at long expirations and present further evidence that makes this claim more plausible.

The SABR Model

Pat Hagan's well-known SABR (or "stochastic alpha beta rho") model (Hagan, Kumar, Lesniewski, and Woodward 2002) has dynamics

$$dS_t = \sigma_t\, S_t^{\beta}\, dZ_1$$
$$d\sigma_t = \chi\, \sigma_t\, dZ_2$$

with $\langle dZ_1\, dZ_2 \rangle = \rho\, dt$.

Volatility does not mean revert in the SABR model, so it is only good for short expirations. Nevertheless the model has the virtue of having an exact expression for the implied volatility smile in the short-expiration limit $\tau \to 0$. The resulting functional form can be used to fit observed short-dated implied volatilities and the model parameters α, β, and ρ thereby extracted. In the special case $\beta = 1$, the SABR implied volatility formula (2.17a) of Hagan, Kumar, Lesniewski, and Woodward (2002) reduces to

$$\sigma_{BS}(k) = \sigma_0\, \frac{y}{f(y)} \left\{ 1 + \left[\frac{1}{4}\, \rho\, \chi\, \sigma_0 + \frac{2 - 3\rho^2}{24}\, \chi^2 \right] \tau + O(\tau^2) \right\} \qquad (7.7)$$

with

$$y := -\chi \frac{k}{\sigma_0}$$

and

$$f(y) = \log\left\{\frac{\sqrt{1 - 2\rho y + y^2} + y - \rho}{1 - \rho}\right\}$$

Note that the lognormal SABR formula (7.7) factorizes with one factor depending only on y and the other factor depending only on τ. Taylor-expanding (7.7) to second order in y and first order in τ (i.e., with $y \sim \sqrt{\tau}$) gives

$$\sigma_{BS}(k,\tau) = \sigma_0 \left\{1 - \frac{1}{2}\rho y + \frac{2 - 3\rho^2}{12} y^2 \right.$$
$$\left. + \left[\frac{1}{4}\rho \chi \sigma_0 + \frac{2 - 3\rho^2}{24} \chi^2\right] \tau + O(\tau\sqrt{\tau})\right\}$$

Substituting $a(\sigma) = 0$ and $b(\sigma) = \chi \sigma_0$ into equation (7.5) give

$$I_1(z;\sigma_0) = \frac{1}{2}\rho \chi \sigma_0 z$$
$$I_2(z;\sigma_0) = \frac{1}{6}\chi^2 \sigma_0 z^2 + \frac{1}{4}\rho \chi \sigma_0^2 + \frac{1}{24}\rho^2 \chi^2 \sigma_0 + \frac{1}{12}\chi^2 \sigma_0 - \frac{1}{6}\rho^2 \chi^2 \sigma_0$$

Then, noting that

$$\chi z \sqrt{\tau} = \chi \frac{k}{\sigma_{BS}} = -y\frac{\sigma_0}{\sigma_{BS}} = -y\left(1 + \frac{1}{2}\rho y\right) + O(y^3)$$

we obtain

$$\sigma_{BS}(k,\tau) = \sigma_0 + I_1(z;\sigma_0)\sqrt{\tau} + I_2(z;\sigma_0)\tau + O(\tau\sqrt{\tau})$$
$$= \sigma_0 \left\{1 - \frac{1}{2}\rho y + \frac{2 - 3\rho^2}{12} y^2 \right.$$
$$\left. + \left[\frac{1}{4}\rho \chi \sigma_0 + \frac{2 - 3\rho^2}{24} \chi^2\right] \tau + O(\tau\sqrt{\tau})\right\}$$

We see that the Medvedev-Scaillet formula (7.5) gives precisely the same result as the SABR implied volatility formula (7.7) for small τ.

Finally, we note that the SABR formula implies that

$$\left.\frac{\partial \sigma_{BS}}{\partial k}\right|_{k=0} = \frac{\rho}{2}$$

which is a special case of the general result (7.6) with $\beta(v) = \sqrt{v}$ and $\eta = 2\chi$. To see this, apply Itô's lemma to the SABR volatility process to obtain

$$dv = \chi^2 v\, dt + 2\chi v\, dZ$$

with $v = \sigma^2$.

INCLUDING JUMPS

Medvedev and Scaillet's (2004) main result is a more complicated expression for models that include jumps in the stock price. The authors note that adding jumps in volatility would make the model more realistic but as we also noted earlier, there is no contribution to the shape of the volatility surface from the jump in volatility for very short expirations.

Specifically, consider the stochastic volatility with jump model

$$\frac{dS_t}{S_t} = \sigma_t\, dZ_1 + J(\sigma_t)\, dq_t$$

$$d\sigma_t = a(\sigma_t)\, dt + b(\sigma_t)\, dZ_2 \qquad (7.8)$$

The jump term dq is a standard Poisson process with intensity $\lambda_J(\sigma_t)$ and $J(\sigma_t)$ is a $(-1, \infty)$-valued random variable with density f sampled at each jump. As before, the jump compensator μ_J is given by

$$\mu_J = \lambda_J \int_{-1}^{+\infty} f(x)\, dx$$

In this model, short-dated implied volatilities are given by

$$I(z, \tau, \sigma) = \sigma + \tilde{I}_1(z; \sigma)\sqrt{\tau} + \tilde{I}_2(z; \sigma)\tau + O(\tau\sqrt{\tau})$$

where $\tilde{I}_1$ and $\tilde{I}_2$ are given by

$$\tilde{I}_1(z; \sigma) = I_1(z; \sigma) - \mu_J\, g(z) + \eta_J\, h(z)$$

$$\tilde{I}_2(z; \sigma) = I_2(z; \sigma) + \frac{1}{2\sigma} \left(\mu_J g(z) - \eta_J h(z) \right)^2 z^2$$

$$- \left\{ -\frac{\mu_J \sigma}{2} - \sigma \lambda_J + \frac{\mu_J^2}{\sigma} + \frac{\mu_J b(\sigma) \rho}{2\sigma} \right\} g(z) z$$

$$- \left\{ \frac{\eta_J \sigma}{2} + \sigma \chi_J - \frac{\mu_J \eta_J}{\sigma} - \frac{\eta_J b(\sigma) \rho}{2\sigma} \right\} h(z) z$$

$$+ \frac{\rho b(\sigma) \mu_J}{2\sigma} - \frac{\rho \partial_\sigma b(\sigma) \mu_J}{2} + \frac{\mu_J^2}{2\sigma} - \frac{\sigma \mu_J}{2} - \lambda_J \sigma \qquad (7.9)$$

where $\eta_J = \lambda_J \int_0^\infty x f(x) \, dx$, $\chi = \lambda_J \int_0^\infty f(x) \, dx$ are respectively the positive part of the jump compensator and the probability of an upwards jump and

$$g(z) = \frac{N(-z)}{N'(z)}; \; h(z) = \frac{1}{N'(z)}$$

As expected, all jump-related terms (with subscript J) vanish if there are no jumps.

Corollaries

In a jump diffusion model (with volatility deterministic), the limit of the implied volatility skew as $\tau \to 0$ is given by

$$\left. \frac{\partial I}{\partial k} \right|_{k=0} \to -\frac{\mu_J}{\sigma}$$

To get this result, note that $g'(0) = 1$ and $h'(0) = 0$. The result is exactly consistent with our earlier heuristic derivation in Chapter 5.

In the SVJ model, the limit of the implied volatility skew as $\tau \to 0$ is given by

$$\left. \frac{\partial I}{\partial k} \right|_{k=0} \to \frac{\rho b(\sigma)}{2\sigma} - \frac{\mu_J}{\sigma}$$

This is consistent with our earlier observation that the jump and stochastic volatility effects on the at-the-money variance skew are approximately additive. In fact we have

$$\left. \frac{\partial v_{BS}}{\partial k} \right|_{k=0} \to \rho b(\sigma) - 2 \mu_J \text{ as } \tau \to 0$$

so they are exactly additive at $\tau = 0$!

LONG EXPIRATIONS: FOUQUE, PAPANICOLAOU, AND SIRCAR

Fouque, Papanicolaou, and Sircar (1999) and Fouque, Papanicolaou, and Sircar (2000) show using a perturbation expansion approach that in any stochastic volatility model where volatility is mean-reverting, Black-Scholes implied volatility can be well approximated by a simple function of log-moneyness and time to expiration for long-dated options. In particular, they study a model where the log-volatility is an Orenstein-Uhlenbeck process (log-OU for short). That is,

$$dx = -\frac{\sigma^2}{2} dt + \sigma \, dZ_1$$

$$d\log(\sigma) = -\lambda [\,\log(\sigma) - \overline{\log(\sigma)}\,]dt + \xi \, dZ_2$$

They find that the slope of the BS implied volatility skew is given (for large λT) by

$$\frac{\partial}{\partial x} \sigma_{BS}(x, T) \approx \frac{\rho \xi}{\lambda T} \qquad (7.10)$$

To recast this in terms of v to be consistent with the form of the generic process we wrote down in equation (7.1), we note that (considering random terms only), $dv \sim 2\,\sigma \, d\sigma$ and in the log-OU model,

$$d\sigma \sim \xi \, \sigma \, dZ_2$$

So

$$dv \sim 2\,\xi \, v \, dZ_2$$

Then $\beta(v)$ as defined in equation (7.1) is given by

$$\eta \, \beta(v) = 2\xi \, \sqrt{v}$$

and, from equation (7.10), the BS implied variance skew is given by

$$\frac{\partial}{\partial x} \sigma_{BS}(x, T)^2 \approx \frac{2\,\rho\,\xi\,\sqrt{v}}{\lambda T} = \frac{\rho\,\eta\,\beta(v)}{\lambda T}$$

Looking back at equation (3.19), we see that the Heston skew (where $\beta(v) = 1$) has the same behavior for large λT. We now have enough evidence to make our generalization more plausible: It seems that both for long and short expirations, the skew behavior may be identical for all stochastic volatility models up to a factor of $\beta(v)$. Supposing this claim were true, what would be the natural way to interpolate the asymptotic skew behaviors between long and short expirations?

Clearly, the most plausible interpolation function between short expiration and long expiration volatility skews is the one we already derived for the Heston model in Chapter 3 and

$$\frac{\partial}{\partial x}\, \sigma_{BS}(x, T)^2 \approx \frac{\rho\, \eta\, \beta(v)}{\lambda'\, T} \left\{ 1 - \frac{\left(1 - e^{-\lambda' T}\right)}{\lambda'\, T} \right\} \tag{7.11}$$

with $\lambda' = \lambda - \frac{1}{2}\rho\, \eta\, \beta(v)$.

SMALL VOLATILITY OF VOLATILITY: LEWIS

Lewis (2000) performs perturbation expansions of implied volatility with respect to the volatility of volatility parameter (assumed small) in any stochastic volatility model of the form (7.1) for general choices of $\beta(v)$.

According to equation (3.14) on p 143 of Lewis (2000), we have

$$v_{BS}(k, t) = \beta_0(v, t) + \beta_1(v, t)\, k + \beta_2(v, t)\, k^2 + O(\eta)^3$$

where

$$\beta_0(v, t) = v + \frac{1}{2}\frac{\eta}{t} J^{(1)} +$$

$$\eta^2 \left[\frac{J^{(2)}}{t} - \frac{1}{2}\frac{J^{(3)}}{v\, t^2} \left(1 + \frac{1}{4} v\, t \right) - \frac{J^{(4)}}{v\, t^2} \left(1 - \frac{1}{4} v\, t \right) \right.$$

$$\left. + \frac{(J^{(1)})^2}{v^2\, t^3} \left(\frac{3}{4} + \frac{1}{16} v\, t \right) \right]$$

$$\beta_1(v, t) = \frac{\eta}{v t^2} J^{(1)} + \eta^2 \left[-\frac{J^{(4)}}{v\, t^2} - \frac{(J^{(1)})^2}{v^2\, t^3} \right]$$

$$\beta_2(v, t) = \eta^2 \left[\frac{1}{2}\frac{J^{(3)}}{v^2\, t^3} + \frac{J^{(4)}}{v^2\, t^3} - \frac{5}{4}\frac{(J^{(1)})^2}{v^3\, t^4} \right] \tag{7.12}$$

Example 4 on page 144 of Lewis (2000) deals with the case of most interest to us:

$$dv = -\lambda \, (v - \bar{v}) \, dt + \eta \, v^\phi \, dZ$$

For this volatility process, in the special case $v = \bar{v}$, we have

$$J^{(1)} = \bar{v}^{1/2+\phi} t \frac{\rho}{\lambda} \left\{ 1 - \frac{1 - e^{-\lambda t}}{\lambda t} \right\}$$

$$J^{(3)} = \bar{v}^{2\phi} \frac{\rho}{2\lambda^3} \left\{ \frac{3}{2} + \lambda t + 2 e^{-\lambda t} - \frac{1}{2} e^{-2\lambda t} \right\}$$

$$J^{(4)} = \bar{v}^{2\phi} \frac{\rho^2}{\lambda^3} \left(\frac{1}{2} + \phi \right) \left\{ -2 + \lambda t + (2 + \lambda t) \, e^{-\lambda t} \right\}$$

Substituting back into equation (7.12) gives

$$\left. \frac{\partial v_{BS}}{\partial k} \right|_{k=0} = \frac{\rho \, \eta \, v^{\phi-1/2}}{\lambda \, t} \left\{ 1 - \frac{1 - e^{-\lambda t}}{\lambda t} \right\} + O(\eta^2)$$

and we see that (7.11) is not only plausible but is exactly correct to first order in the volatility of volatility η.

EXTREME STRIKES: ROGER LEE

In a beautiful paper, Roger Lee (2004) shows that implied variance is bounded above by a function linear in the log-strike $k = \log(K/F)$ as $|k| \to \infty$. Moreover, he shows how to relate the gradients of the wings of the upper bound of the implied variance skew to the maximal finite moments of the underlying process.

Specifically, let $q^* := \sup \left\{ q : \mathbb{E} \, S_T^{-q} < \infty \right\}$ and

$$\beta^* := \limsup_{k \to -\infty} \frac{\sigma_{BS}^2(k, T) \, T}{|k|}$$

Then $\beta^* \in [0, 2]$,

$$q^* = \frac{1}{2} \left(\frac{1}{\sqrt{\beta^*}} - \frac{\sqrt{\beta^*}}{2} \right)^2$$

and inverting this, we obtain $\beta^* = g(q^*)$ with

$$g(x) = 2 - 4 \left[\sqrt{x^2 + x} - x \right]$$

Also let $p^* := \sup \left\{ p : \mathbb{E} \, S_T^{1+p} < \infty \right\}$ and

$$\alpha^* := \limsup_{k \to +\infty} \frac{\sigma_{BS}^2(k, T) \, T}{|k|}$$

Then $\alpha^* \in [0, 2]$,

$$p^* = \frac{1}{2} \left(\frac{1}{\sqrt{\alpha^*}} - \frac{\sqrt{\alpha^*}}{2} \right)^2$$

and as for the left wing, it follows that $\alpha^* = g(p^*)$.

Lee's derivation assumes only the existence of a Martingale measure: It makes no assumptions on the distribution of underlying returns. His result is completely model independent.

Denote the (cumulative) distribution function of the returns x of the underlying by $F(x)$. Benaim and Friz (2006) go on to show that Roger Lee's upper bound (lim sup) may be replaced by a limit provided that $\log [1 - F(x)]$ and $\log [F(-x)]$ respectively satisfy some technical conditions that are in fact satisfied in most models of practical interest. If so, we may write for the right tail

$$\frac{\sigma_{BS}(k, T)^2 \, T}{k} \sim g \left(-1 - \frac{\log [1 - F(k)]}{k} \right) \quad \text{as } k \to \infty \qquad (7.13)$$

and for the left tail

$$\frac{\sigma_{BS}(-k, T)^2 \, T}{k} \sim g \left(\frac{-\log F(-k)}{k} \right) \quad \text{as } k \to \infty \qquad (7.14)$$

So, by direct substitution of the tail behavior of the distribution F of underlying returns into equations (7.13) and (7.14), we can deduce the full tail behavior of the smile, not just Lee's upper bound. Moreover, the tail behavior of the distribution is known for a large class of models.

The connection between the Lee and Benaim-Friz results becomes clear when we note that in most models of practical interest, the limits exist,

$$q^* = \lim_{k \to \infty} \left\{ -\frac{\log F(-k)}{k} \right\}$$

and

$$p^* = \lim_{k \to \infty} \left\{ -1 - \frac{\log\left[1 - F(k)\right]}{k} \right\}$$

Example: Black-Scholes

In the Black-Scholes case with time to expiration T and volatility σ,

$$1 - F(k) = \int_k^\infty \frac{1}{\sqrt{2\pi\sigma^2 T}} e^{-y^2/(2\sigma^2 T)} \, dy \sim \frac{1}{\sqrt{2\pi}} \frac{e^{-k^2/(2\sigma^2 T)}}{k} \text{ as } k \to \infty$$

Then

$$\log\left[1 - F(k)\right] \sim -\frac{k^2}{2\sigma^2 T} \text{ as } k \to \infty$$

and

$$\frac{\sigma_{BS}(k, T)^2 T}{k} \sim g\left(-1 + \frac{k}{2\sigma^2 T}\right) \sim \frac{2\sigma^2 T}{2k} \text{ as } k \to \infty$$

It follows that

$$\sigma_{BS}(k, T)^2 \sim \sigma^2 \text{ as } k \to \infty$$

in trivial agreement with the Black-Scholes flat volatility smile. Note that we obtain the full limiting behavior from the Benaim-Friz result; in the Black-Scholes case, all moments are finite, $p^* = q^* = \infty$ and the lim sup result does not exclude behavior $\sim k/\log(k)$ for example.

Stochastic Volatility Models

Drăgulescu and Yakovenko (2002) compute the tail behavior of the Heston cumulative distribution function and find it to be linear in $|k|$. It follows from Benaim and Friz that the tail behavior of $\sigma_{BS}^2(k, T)$ must also be linear in $|k|$. As noted by Drăgulescu and Yakovenko, qualitatively similar results from other authors suggest that linearity in the tails is a generic feature of stochastic volatility models, not just the Heston model.

ASYMPTOTICS IN SUMMARY

It's quite clear from the results presented here that the general shape of the volatility surface doesn't depend very much on the specific choice of model. Any stochastic volatility with jump model should generate a similar shape of volatility surface with appropriate numerical choices of the parameters.

CHAPTER 8

Dynamics of the Volatility Surface

I n Chapter 7, we saw that all stochastic volatility models have essentially the same implications for the shape of the volatility surface. At first it might seem that it would be hard to differentiate between models. That would certainly be the case if we were to confine our attention to the shape of the volatility surface today. However, if instead we were to study the dynamics of the volatility skew—in particular, how the observed volatility skew depends on the overall level of volatility, we would be able to differentiate between models.

DYNAMICS OF THE VOLATILITY SKEW
UNDER STOCHASTIC VOLATILITY

Empirical studies of the dynamics of the volatility skew show that $\frac{\partial}{\partial k}\sigma(k,t)$ is approximately independent of volatility level over time. Translating this into a statement about the implied variance skew, we get

$$\frac{\partial}{\partial k}\,\sigma_{BS}(k,t)^2 = 2\,\sigma_{BS}(k,t)\,\frac{\partial}{\partial k}\,\sigma_{BS}(k,t) \sim \sqrt{v(k,t)}.$$

Comparing this with equation (7.11), we see that this in turn implies that $\beta(v) \sim \sqrt{v}$. Referring back to the definition of $\beta(v)$ (7.1), we conclude that v is approximately lognormal in contrast to the square root process assumed by Heston. This makes intuitive sense given that we would expect volatility to be more volatile if the volatility level is high than if the volatility level itself is low.

Does it matter whether we model variance as a square root process or as lognormal? In certain cases it does. After all, we are using our model to hedge and the hedge should approximately generate the correct payoff at the boundary. If the payoff that we are hedging depends (directly or indirectly) on the volatility skew, and our assumption is that the variance skew is independent of the volatility level, we could end up losing a lot of money if that's not how the market actually behaves.

Is any stochastic volatility model better than none at all? The answer here has to be yes because, whereas having the wrong stochastic volatility model will cause the hedger to generate a payoff corresponding to a skew that may be off by a factor of 1.5 if volatility doubles, having only a local volatility model will cause the hedger to generate a payoff that corresponds to almost no forward skew at all. We now show this.

DYNAMICS OF THE VOLATILITY SKEW UNDER LOCAL VOLATILITY

Empirically, the slope of the volatility skew decreases with time to expiration. From the above, in the case of mean-reverting stochastic volatility, the term structure of the BS implied variance skew will look something like equation (7.11). In particular, the slope of the volatility skew decays over time according to the time behavior of the coefficient

$$\frac{1}{\lambda' T} \left\{ 1 - \frac{\left(1 - e^{-\lambda' T}\right)}{\lambda' T} \right\}$$

Recall from Chapter 1 the formula (1.10) for local volatility in terms of implied volatility:

$$v_{loc} = \frac{\frac{\partial w}{\partial T}}{1 - \frac{k}{w}\frac{\partial w}{\partial k} + \frac{1}{4}\left(-\frac{1}{4} - \frac{1}{w} + \frac{k^2}{w}^2\right)\left(\frac{\partial w}{\partial k}\right)^2 + \frac{1}{2}\frac{\partial^2 w}{\partial k^2}}$$

Differentiating with respect to x and considering only the leading term in $\frac{\partial w}{\partial k}$ (which is small for large T), we find

$$\frac{\partial v_{loc}}{\partial k} \approx \frac{\partial}{\partial T}\frac{\partial w}{\partial k} + \frac{1}{w}\frac{\partial w}{\partial T}\frac{\partial w}{\partial k}$$

That is, the local variance skew $\frac{\partial v_{loc}}{\partial k}$ decays with the BS implied total variance skew $\frac{\partial w}{\partial k}$.

To get the forward volatility surface from the local volatility surface in a local volatility model, we integrate over the local volatilities from the (forward) valuation date to the expiration of the option along the most probable path joining the current stock price to the strike price using the trick presented in Chapter 3. It is obvious that the forward implied volatility surface is substantially flatter than today's because the forward local volatility skews are all flatter.

Contrast this with a stochastic volatility model where implied volatility skews are approximately time-homogeneous. In other words, local volatility models imply that future BS implied volatility surfaces will be flat (relative to today's) and stochastic volatility models imply that future BS implied volatility surfaces will look like today's.

STOCHASTIC IMPLIED VOLATILITY MODELS

Many authors including Brace, Goldys, Klebaner, and Womersley (2001), Cont and da Fonseca (2002), Ledoit, Santa-Clara, and Yan (2002) and Schönbucher (1999) have looked at models that allow the entire implied volatility surface to diffuse. It turns out that if the underlying price process is assumed continuous (with no jumps), the statics and dynamics of the implied volatility surface are highly constrained.

In particular, nondiscounted option prices are risk-neutral expectations of future cashflows and as such must be martingales. Changes in the call price reflect changes in the underlying and changes in implied volatility. Imposing the martingale constraint

$$\mathbb{E}[dC_t] = 0$$

gives a tight relationship between the various sensitivities and many results such as equation (7.3) follow immediately from this.

More recently, Durrleman (2005) showed how to extract the dynamics of instantaneous variance from the dynamics of the observed implied volatility surface in the limit of very short expirations and very close to at-the-money. Conversely, given a stochastic volatility model, he showed how to deduce the shape of the implied volatility surface in that same neighborhood. However, to get these impressive results, one has to assume continuity of the underlying price process but as we have seen earlier, jumps in the underlying are needed to explain the shape of the implied volatility surface. Moreover, as noted by Cont, da Fonseca, and Durrleman (2002) and as observed by any option trader, there appear to be jumps in the implied volatility surface too.

DIGITAL OPTIONS AND DIGITAL CLIQUETS

Applying our insights to the valuation of actual derivative contracts, we choose to study digital options because their valuation involves the volatility skew directly.

Valuing Digital Options

A digital (call) option $D(K, T)$ pays 1 if the stock price S_T at expiration T is greater than the strike price K and zero otherwise. It may be valued as the limit of a call spread as the spread between the strikes is reduced to zero.

$$D(K, T) = -\frac{\partial C(K, T)}{\partial K} \tag{8.1}$$

where $C(K, T)$ represents the price of a European call option with strike K expiring at time T.

To see that its price is very sensitive to the volatility skew, we rewrite the European call price in equation (8.1) in terms of its Black-Scholes implied volatility $\sigma_{BS}(K, T)$.

$$
\begin{aligned}
D(K, T) &= -\frac{\partial}{\partial K} C_{BS}\left(K, T, \sigma_{BS}(K, T)\right) \\
&= -\frac{\partial C_{BS}}{\partial K} - \frac{\partial C_{BS}}{\partial \sigma_{BS}} \frac{\partial \sigma_{BS}}{\partial K}
\end{aligned}
$$

To get an idea of the impact of the skew in practice, consider our usual idealized market with zero interest rate and dividends and a one-year digital option struck at-the-money. Suppose further that at-the-money volatility is 25% and the volatility skew (typical of SPX for example) is 3% per 10% change in strike. Its value is given by

$$
\begin{aligned}
D(1, 1) &= -\frac{\partial C_{BS}}{\partial K} - \frac{\partial C_{BS}}{\partial \sigma_{BS}} \frac{\partial \sigma_{BS}}{\partial K} \\
&= N\left(-\frac{\sigma}{2}\right) - \text{vega} \times \text{skew} \\
&= N\left(-\frac{\sigma}{2}\right) + \frac{1}{\sqrt{2\pi}} e^{-\frac{d_1^2}{2}} \times 0.3 \\
&\approx N\left(-\frac{\sigma}{2}\right) + 0.4 \times 0.3
\end{aligned}
$$

If we had ignored the skew contribution, we would have got the price of the digital option wrong by 12% of notional!

Digital Cliquets

Here is part of a definition of the word cliquet from the Dictionary of Financial Risk Management (Gastineau and Kritzman 1999):

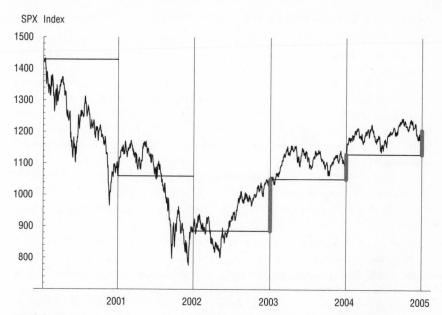

FIGURE 8.1 Illustration of a cliquet payoff. This hypothetical SPX cliquet resets at-the-money every year on October 31. The thick solid lines represent nonzero cliquet payoffs. The payoff of a 5-year European option struck at the October 31, 2000, SPX level of 1429.40 would have been zero.

> The French like the sound of "cliquet" and seem prepared to apply the term to any remotely appropriate option structure. (1) Originally a periodic reset option with multiple payouts or a ratchet option (from vilbrequin à cliquet—ratchet brace). Also called Ratchet Option ...

Since the word is originally French, here is an elegant definition of the "Effet-cliquet" from the French Web site http://lexique-financier. actufinance.fr:

> Mécanisme qui permet de figer une performance même si l'actif correspondant baisse par la suite.*

The payoff of a hypothetical cliquet contract is shown in Figure 8.1.

For our purposes, a cliquet is just a series of options whose strikes are set on a sequence of future dates. In particular, a digital cliquet is a sequence of

---

*Mechanism that permits a profit to be locked in even if the underlying subsequently declines.

digital options whose strikes will be set (usually) at the prevailing stock price on the relevant reset date. Denoting the set of reset dates by $\{t_1, t_2, \ldots, t_n\}$, the digital cliquet pays Coupon $\times \theta\left(S_{t_i} - S_{t_{i-1}}\right)$ at t_i where $\theta(.)$ represents the Heaviside function.

One can see immediately that the package consisting of a zero coupon bond together with a digital cliquet makes a very natural product for a risk-averse retail investor—he or she typically gets an above-market coupon if the underlying stock index is up for the period (usually a year) and a below-market coupon (usually zero) if the underlying stock index is down. Not surprisingly, this product was and is very popular and as a result, many equity derivatives dealers have digital cliquets on their books.

From the foregoing, the price of a digital cliquet may vary very substantially depending on the modeling assumptions made by the seller. Those sellers using local volatility models will certainly value a digital cliquet at a lower price than sellers using a stochastic volatility (or more practically, those guessing that the forward skew should look like today's). Perversely then, those sellers using an inadequate model will almost certainly win the deal and end up short a portfolio of misvalued forward-starting digital options. Or even worse, a dealer could have an appropriate valuation approach but be pushed internally by the salespeople to match (mistaken) competitors' lower prices.

How wrong could the price of the digital cliquet be? Consider the example of a (not unrealistic) five-year deal that has a 6% coupon annually if the underlying exceeds the prior annual setting and zero otherwise. Neglecting the first coupon (because we suppose that all dealers can price a digital which sets today), the error could be up to 12% of the sum of the remaining coupons (48%) or 5.76% of Notional. A pricing error of this magnitude is a big multiple of the typical margin on such a trade and would cause the dealer a substantial loss.

CHAPTER 9

Barrier Options

Barrier options are important building blocks for structured products, but their valuation can be highly model dependent. Consequently much has been written on the subject, notably by Taleb (1996), Wilmott (2000) and Carr and Chou (1997).

Despite all the existing literature, convincing barrier option solutions are thin on the ground. In fact, prices quoted for certain kinds of barrier option can vary so much between dealers that customers can sometimes cross the bid-offer (that is, buy on one dealer's offer and sell on another dealer's bid for a profit). So there is still plenty of scope for the ambitious modeler.

By considering two limiting cases, we see that barrier option values are not always very model dependent. However, the valuation of certain types of barrier options can be extremely model dependent. Developing intuition is therefore particularly important not only to be able to estimate the value of a barrier options but also to know whether the output of a model should be trusted or not. Accordingly, we will use the insights gained from earlier chapters to understand the relative pricing of various types of barrier options under stochastic and local volatility dynamics.

As usual, we suppose that European options of all strikes and expirations are traded in the market and our objective is to price barrier options consistently with these European option prices.

DEFINITIONS

A *knock-out* option is an option that becomes worthless when a prespecified "barrier" level is reached.

A *live-out* option is a special case of a knock-out option that is significantly in-the-money when it knocks out.

A *knock-in* option is an option that can only be exercised if a barrier level is reached prior to exercise. Obviously, a knock-in option is just a portfolio of short a knock-out option and long a European.

An amount of money paid to a barrier option buyer if the barrier is hit is termed a *rebate*. This rebate may be paid when the barrier is hit or at expiration.

LIMITING CASES

Limit Orders

Suppose we sell a knock-out call option with barrier B equal to the strike price K below the current stock price S. Suppose further that we hedge this position by buying one stock per option and we charge $S_0 - K$ as the premium. If interest rates and dividends are zero, it is clear that this hedge is perfect. To see this, suppose first that the barrier is never hit: The buyer of the knock-out call option exercises the option and we deliver the stock. Net proceeds are $-(S_T - K) + (S_0 - K) + (S_T - S_0) = 0$. On the other hand, if the barrier is hit, we lose $S_0 - K$ on our purchase of stock which is perfectly offset by the premium we charged.

In this special case, a knock-out option has no optionality whatsoever. Delta is one, gamma is zero, and vega is zero. The result is completely model independent; the only requirement is to have no carry on the stock for this construction to work.

Now consider what this portfolio really is. So long as the stock price remains above the barrier level, we are net flat. When the barrier is hit, the option knocks out and we are left long of the stock we bought to hedge. This is exactly the portfolio we would have if the option buyer had left us a stop-loss order to sell stock if the price ever reached the barrier level B. There is however a big difference between the two contracts—a barrier option like this guarantees execution at the barrier level but a conventional stop-loss order would get filled at the earliest opportunity after the barrier is hit (usually a bit below the barrier). If we could really trade continuously as models conventionally assume, there would be no difference between the two contracts. In the real world, a knock-out option needs to be priced more highly than the model price to compensate for the risk of the stock price gapping through the barrier level. Practitioners compensate for gap risk when pricing options by moving the barrier by some amount related to the expected gap in the stock price when the barrier is hit.

In summary, in this special case when $K = B < S_0$, the price of a knock-out call is given by the difference $S_0 - K$ between the current stock price and the strike price plus a bit to compensate for gap risk.

Now, if the strike price K and the barrier level B are not equal but not so far apart with $B \leq K \leq S_0$, it is natural to expect that neither gamma nor vega would be very high relative to the European option with the same strike K. Nor would we expect the price of such a knock-out option to be very sensitive to the model used to value it (assuming of course that this model prices consistently with all European options). Investigation shows that this is indeed the case.

European Capped Calls

The next limiting case we consider is that of the European capped call. This option is a call struck at K with barrier $B > S_0$ such that if the stock price reaches B before expiration, the option expires and pays out intrinsic of $B - K$.

If the barrier is far away from the current stock price S_0, the price of such an option cannot be very different from the price of a conventional European option. To see this, consider a portfolio consisting of a long European option struck at K (not too different from S_0) and short the capped call. If the barrier is not hit, this portfolio pays nothing. If the barrier is hit, the portfolio will be long a European option and short cash in the amount of the intrinsic value $B - K$. The time value of this European option cannot be very high because, by assumption, $B \gg S_0$ and moreover, the barrier is most likely to be hit close to expiration. Since the value of the capped call must be close to the value of a conventional European call, the value of the capped call cannot be very model dependent and should be well approximated by a model using Black-Scholes assumptions (no volatility skew) and the implied volatility of the corresponding European option.

With this understanding of the pricing of capped calls, we are in a position to develop intuition for the pricing of live-out calls. To get a live-out call from a capped call, we need only omit the rebate at the barrier. We would then have a call option struck at K that goes deep-in-the-money as the stock price approaches the barrier $B \gg K$ and knocks out when the stock price reaches B (with no rebate). So to get intuition for the pricing and hedging of live-out options, we need only study the pricing and hedging of the rebate (or *one-touch* option).

THE REFLECTION PRINCIPLE

We suppose that the stock price is driven by a constant volatility stochastic process with zero log-drift. That is

$$dx = \sigma \, dZ \tag{9.1}$$

with $x := \log (S/K)$.

In this special case, there is a very simple relationship between the price of a European binary option struck at B and the value of the one-touch option struck at B.

Consider the realization of the zero log-drift stochastic process (9.1) given by the solid line in Figure 9.1. From the symmetry of the problem, the dashed path has the same probability of being realized as the original solid path. We deduce that the probability of hitting the barrier B is exactly twice the probability of ending up below the barrier at expiration. Putting this another way, the value of a one-touch option is precisely twice the value of a European binary put.

To make this result appear plausible note that an at-the-money barrier has 100% chance of getting hit but there is only 50% chance of ending up below the barrier at expiration in this special case. Guessing at a generalization, we might suppose that the ratio of the fair value of a one-touch option should be given by $B(S_0)^{-1}$ where $B(K)$ represents the value of a European binary put struck at K.

If this guess were correct, for the Heston-Nandi model and parameters of Chapter 4 $(v = 0.04, \bar{v} = 0.04, \lambda = 10, \eta = 1, \rho = -1)$, where $B(S_0) = 0.54614$, the ratio of the one-touch price to the European binary price should be around $B(S_0)^{-1} = 1.831$. Figure 9.2 shows how this ratio is, as Taleb (1996) emphasizes, very sensitive to modeling assumptions. Although our guess is pretty accurate for the local volatility case, it is very inaccurate in the stochastic volatility case.

For comparison, consider the effect of modeling assumptions on the price of a European binary call. Figure 9.3 shows that modeling assumptions

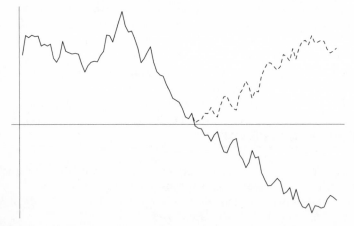

FIGURE 9.1   A realization of the zero log-drift stochastic process and the reflected path.

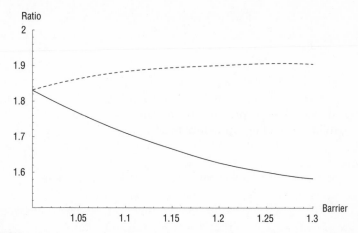

FIGURE 9.2 The ratio of the value of a one-touch call to the value of a European binary call under stochastic volatility and local volatility assumptions as a function of strike. The solid line is stochastic volatility and the dashed line is local volatility.

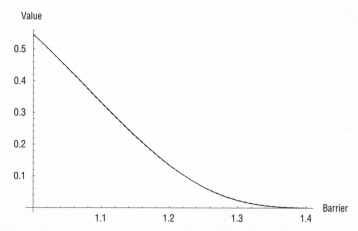

FIGURE 9.3 The value of a European binary call under stochastic volatility and local volatility assumptions as a function of strike. The solid line is stochastic volatility and the dashed line is local volatility. The two lines are almost indistinguishable.

have no effect—the price of a European binary is independent of modeling assumptions and depends only on the given prices of conventional European options (being a limit of a call spread in this case).

Finally, we graph the value of the one-touch option as a function of strike under stochastic volatility and local volatility assumptions in Figure 9.4.

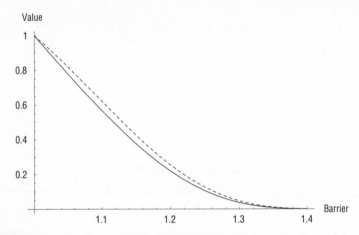

FIGURE 9.4   The value of a one-touch call under stochastic volatility and local volatility assumptions as a function of barrier level. The solid line is stochastic volatility and the dashed line is local volatility.

THE LOOKBACK HEDGING ARGUMENT

A closely related useful hedging argument originally given by Goldman, Sosin, and Gatto (1979) is used to estimate the price and hedge portfolio of a lookback option. For our purposes, we define a lookback call to be an option that pays $(\tilde{S} - K)^+$ at expiration where $\tilde{S}$ is the maximum stock price over the life of the option and K is the strike price.

Once again, assuming zero log-drift and constant volatility, suppose we hedge a short position in this lookback call by holding two conventional European options struck at K. If the stock price never reaches K, both the lookback and the European option expire worthless. If and when the stock price does reach K and increases by some small increment ΔK, the value of the lookback option must increase by ΔK (since $K + \Delta K$ is now the new maximum). The new lookback option must pay $\Delta K + (\tilde{S} - (K + \Delta K))^+$ — the payoff of another lookback option with a higher strike price plus a fixed cashflow ΔK.

Assuming we were right to hedge with two calls in the first place, the new hedge portfolio must be two calls struck at $K + \Delta K$. So we must rebalance our hedge portfolio by selling two calls struck at K and buying two calls struck at $K + \Delta K$. The profit generated by rebalancing is

$$2\,C(K + \Delta K, K) - 2\,C(K + \Delta K, K + \Delta K) \approx -2\left.\frac{\partial C}{\partial K}\right|_{S=K}\Delta K$$

$$= 2\,N\,(d_2)\big|_{S=K}\,\Delta K$$

$$= \Delta K$$

using the fact that $N\,(d_2)\big|_{S=K} = 1/2$ when the log-drift is zero.

The profit generated by rebalancing is exactly what is needed to generate the required payoff of the lookback option and our hedge is perfect.

One-Touch Options Again

Now reconsider the value of a one-touch call option struck at B. It is the probability that the maximum stock price is greater than B. We can generate this payoff by taking the limit of a lookback call spread as the difference between the strikes gets very small. Because a lookback call has the same value as two European calls, a lookback call spread must have the same value as two European call spreads. Put another way, a one-touch option is worth two European binary options when the log-drift is zero.

PUT-CALL SYMMETRY

We now assume zero interest rates and dividends and constant volatility again (as opposed to zero log-drift). In this case, by inspection of the Black-Scholes formula, we have

$$C\left(\frac{B^2}{S}, K\right) = \frac{K}{S}\,P\left(S, \frac{B^2}{K}\right)$$

From one of the many references containing closed-form formulas for knock-out options, we may deduce that

$$DO\,(S, K, B) = C\,(S, K) - \frac{S}{B}\,C\left(\frac{B^2}{S}, K\right)$$

$$= C\,(S, K) - \frac{K}{B}\,P\left(S, \frac{B^2}{K}\right)$$

where $DO(.)$ represents the value of a down-and-out call.

By letting $S = B$ in the above formula, we see that $DO\,(B, K, B) = 0$ as we would expect. So, in this special case, there is a static hedge for a down-and-out call option that consists of long a European call with the same strike and short $\frac{K}{B}$ European puts struck at the reflection of the log-strike in the log-barrier ($K' = B^2/K$).

The reason this static hedge works is that the value of the call we are long always exactly offsets the value of the put we are short when the stock price reaches the barrier B.

A special case of this special case is when $B = K$. In this case, we have

$$DO\,(S, K, K) = C\,(S, K) - P\,(S, K) = S - K$$

and we see again that there is no optionality—the down-and-out call option is worth only intrinsic value and has the same payoff as a portfolio of long the stock and short K bonds as we argued before.

QUASISTATIC HEDGING AND QUALITATIVE VALUATION

We can generalize the static hedging procedure of the previous section to other cases where interest rates, dividends and volatility have arbitrary structure. Although there is no exact static hedge in the general case, we can construct a portfolio that has rather small payoffs under all reasonable scenarios.

A sophisticated version of this procedure known as the Lagrangian Uncertain Volatility Model is described by Avellaneda, Levy, and Parás (1995). In this model, volatility is bounded but uncertain; volatility is assumed to be high when the portfolio is short gamma and low when the portfolio is long gamma (worst case). Thus, different prices are generated depending on whether an option position is long or short (a bid-offer spread is generated). By minimizing the bid-offer spread of a given portfolio of exotic options (such as barrier options) and European options with respect to the weights of the European options, we can determine an optimal hedge and the minimal bid-offer spread that would be required to guarantee profitability assuming that volatility does indeed remain within the assumed bounds.

More practically, we can use the quasi-static hedging idea to determine the impact of modeling assumptions on the valuation of any given barrier-like claim. The idea is to first determine what the quasistatic hedge looks like, then figure out how this hedge behaves under various future stock price and volatility scenarios—a sort of mental Monte Carlo simulation. We now illustrate this approach with a few examples.

Out-of-the-Money Barrier Options

For concreteness, suppose we sell a call with strike K that knocks out at $B < K$. In this case, the quasistatic hedge portfolio is long a European call

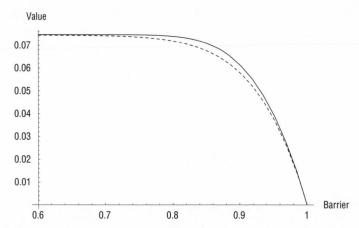

FIGURE 9.5 Values of knock-out call options struck at 1 as a function of barrier level. The solid line is stochastic volatility; the dashed line is local volatility.

with strike K and short an out-of-the money European put (with strike B^2/K in the zero log-drift case).

If the barrier is never hit, the hedge is obviously good. On the other hand, if the barrier is hit, the value of the then out-of-the-money European call and out-of-the-money European put in the hedge portfolio depend on the then volatility skew. From our discussion of volatility surface dynamics in Chapter 8, we know that with the Heston-Nandi parameters of Chapter 4, the skew will be flatter (less negative) under local volatility than under stochastic volatility. We conclude that when the barrier is hit, the hedge portfolio will be worth *more* under local volatility than under stochastic volatility. However, both options will be out-of-the-money so we don't expect the skew effect to be very big. We therefore guess that the pricing of a call that knocks out out-of-the-money would be a little lower under local volatility (because the net expected hedging cost is lower) than under stochastic volatility. This guess is supported by the graphs in Figures 9.5 and 9.6.

One-Touch Options

Recall that a one-touch call option pays some prespecified amount of money if an upside barrier is hit. Suppose we sell such a one-touch call option struck at $B > S$. The quasi-static hedge portfolio should be (approximately) long a strip of European binary call options struck at B. Once again, if the barrier is never hit, the hedge is obviously fine. With the Heston-Nandi

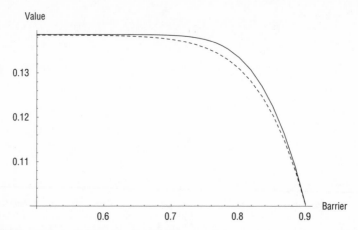

FIGURE 9.6 Values of knock-out call options struck at 0.9 as a function of barrier level. The solid line is stochastic volatility; the dashed line is local volatility.

parameters of Chapter 4,* the skew when the barrier is hit will be flatter (less negative) under local volatility than under stochastic volatility. It follows that the binary call options will be worth *more* under stochastic volatility. That is, on average the one-touch option costs less to hedge under stochastic volatility than under local volatility and so its upfront valuation should be lower under stochastic volatility. This qualitative argument explains the graph shown in Figure 9.4.

Live-Out Options

As before, we model a live-out call as a capped call minus a one-touch. Once again, we guess that the value of the capped call should be pretty much identical under stochastic and local volatility modeling assumptions. On the other hand, from our previous discussion, with the Heston-Nandi parameters of Chapter 4, we expect the value of the one-touch option to be lower under stochastic volatility than under local volatility.

We conclude that with these parameters, a live-out call should be worth *more* under stochastic volatility than under local volatility. This guess is supported by the graph in Figure 9.7. Note that the difference in valuation between the two modeling assumptions can be *very substantial.*

---

*The implication here and in what follows is that where some result is shown to hold for this special choice of parameters that make computations easy, there is every reason to suppose that the same result holds more generally for any choice of stochastic volatility dynamics and parameters.

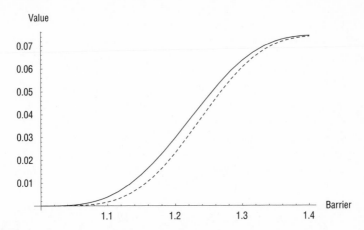

FIGURE 9.7   Values of live-out call options struck at 1 as a function of barrier level. The solid line is stochastic volatility; the dashed line is local volatility.

Lookback Options

Suppose now that we sell a lookback call option struck at $K > S$. The hedge is roughly two European call options struck at K. If the stock price never reaches K, the hedge is fine. If and when the stock price reaches K, we need to sell our two European calls with strike K and buy two new calls with strike $K + \Delta K$. Equivalently, we need to sell two call spreads. Once again, with the Heston-Nandi parameters of Chapter 4, the skew will be more negative under stochastic volatility than under local volatility. We therefore earn more for our call spreads under stochastic volatility than under local volatility. We conclude that with these parameters, a lookback call option should be valued lower under stochastic volatility than under local volatility assumptions. This guess is supported by the graph in Figure 9.8. On closer examination, we see that the ratio of the stochastic volatility value to the local volatility value decreases with increasing strike. That's because on average the higher the strike, the greater the time elapsed between inception and the first rebalancing operation.

ADJUSTING FOR DISCRETE MONITORING

A practical point that is worth noting is that the discreteness effect for barrier options is very significant. Often barrier option contracts specify that the barrier is only to be monitored at the market close. How can we estimate the magnitude of the effect of this on the value of a barrier option?

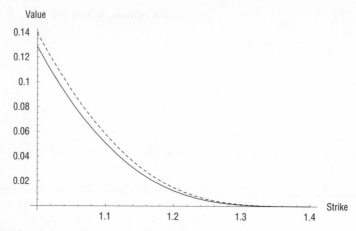

FIGURE 9.8 Values of lookback call options as a function of strike. The solid line is stochastic volatility; the dashed line is local volatility.

We can get an idea of the order of magnitude of the correction using our newly acquired intuition for lookback options. Without loss of generality, suppose a given discrete (up-) barrier option is monitored daily and consider the day on which the discrete maximum is first reached. It is highly likely that the continuous maximum was reached on the same day. At the beginning of that day, the expected difference between the maximum reached and the final stock price is a lookback option that is worth approximately twice a 1-day European option or

$$2 \frac{\sigma \sqrt{\Delta T}}{\sqrt{2\pi}} \approx 0.8 \, \sigma \sqrt{\Delta T}$$

Then, denoting the fair value of discretely monitored and continuously monitored options with up-barrier B by $\tilde{V}(B)$ and $V(B)$ respectively, we have

$$\tilde{V}(B) \approx V\left(B \, e^{0.8 \, \sigma \sqrt{\Delta T}}\right)$$

In fact, Broadie, Glasserman, and Kou (1999) prove the following theorem:

Let $V(B)$ be the price of a continuous barrier option, and $V_m(B)$ be the price of an otherwise identical barrier option with m monitoring points. Then we have the approximation

$$V_m(B) = V(B \, e^{\pm \beta \sigma \sqrt{T/m}}) + o(1/\sqrt{m})$$

with + for an up option and − for a down option, where the constant

$$\beta = -\frac{\zeta(1/2)}{\sqrt{2\pi}} \approx 0.5826$$

and ζ is the Riemann zeta function.

The idea of the proof is to estimate the amount by which the discretely monitored stock price overshoots the barrier level (as it must in general) the first time it exceeds it. The amount of overshoot is given approximately by $B\,e^{\pm\beta\sigma\sqrt{T/m}} - B$.

The difference in price between a discretely monitored barrier option and its continuously monitored equivalent is often substantial. For example, with $\sigma = 0.32$ and daily monitoring ($\sqrt{\Delta T} \approx 1/16$), the adjustment would be around $\frac{0.32 \times 0.6}{16} = .012$ (1.2% of the barrier level).

Discretely Monitored Lookback Options

One might guess from the previous result that the expected difference between the continuous maximum and the discrete maximum might be approximated by the same number. Broadie, Glasserman, and Kou (1999) prove that this is indeed the case. In their paper they show that

$$\mathbb{E}[\hat{S}_T] = \mathbb{E}[\tilde{S}_T]\,e^{-\beta\sigma\sqrt{\Delta T}} \qquad (9.2)$$

where $\hat{S}$ is the discrete maximum, $\tilde{S}$ is the continuous maximum and ΔT is the monitoring interval.

An at-the-money lookback (or hindsight) option $\hat{L}(S_0, T)$ pays the discrete maximum minus the initial stock price. We can rewrite equation (9.2) as

$$
\begin{aligned}
\hat{L}(S_0, T) &= \mathbb{E}[\hat{S}_T - S_0] \\
&= \mathbb{E}[\tilde{S}_T]\,e^{-\beta\sigma\sqrt{\Delta T}} - S_0 \\
&= \tilde{L}(S_0\,e^{-\beta\sigma\sqrt{\Delta T}}, T) - S_0\left(1 - e^{-\beta\sigma\sqrt{\Delta T}}\right)
\end{aligned}
$$

where $\tilde{L}$ is the equivalent continuously monitored option. Similar adjustments for other types of lookback option are given in the (Broadie, Glasserman, and Kou 1999).

PARISIAN OPTIONS

As described in Taleb (1996), continuously monitored barrier options can tempt either the option buyer or seller to influence the underlying stock price ("barrier wars"). Discretely monitored options suffer from similar problems. One way to retain the benefits of barrier options while minimizing the risk of manipulation is to specify that in order for the option to knock-in (or out as the case may be), the underlying stock price must stay outside the barrier for a minimum period of time referred to as a *window*. In this case, the option is called a *Parisian* option. As a further advantage, Parisian options have much less extreme greeks than their non-Parisian counterparts.

Parisian-style features are common in convertible bonds and whenever the size of a derivative is large relative to the liquidity of the underlying stock.

With the usual constant parameter assumptions, Parisian options can be valued in almost-closed form by applying some results on the excursion process of Brownian motion (see for example Chapter 12 of Revuz and Yor (1999)). However in the general case, as in most other barrier option valuation problems, the most natural valuation approach is numerical PDE as described for example by Tavella and Randall (2000).

SOME APPLICATIONS OF BARRIER OPTIONS

Ladders

Consider a strip of capped calls with strikes B_i strictly increasing and greater than the initial stock price S_0. The cap of the option with strike B_i is B_{i+1} so a rebate of $B_{i+1} - B_i$ is paid when the barrier at B_{i+1} is hit. The buyer of such an option locks in his gain each time a barrier is crossed. This gain is not lost if the stock price subsequently falls. Not surprisingly, this structure is very popular with retail investors. In the limit where the caps are very close to the strikes, a ladder approximates a lookback option (every time the stock price increases, the gain is locked in) and the value of the ladder would be approximately twice the value of a European option. Typically though, barriers would be every 10% or so and the value of the ladder would be around 1.5 times the value of the corresponding European option.

Ranges

Another popular investment is one that pays a high coupon for each day that the stock price remains within a range but ceases paying a coupon as soon as one of the boundaries is hit. This is a just a one-touch double barrier construction.

CONCLUSION

Barrier option values can be very sensitive to modeling assumptions and prices must be adjusted to take this into account. Nevertheless, by understanding limiting cases that are well understood, we can gain a good qualitative understanding of the appropriate valuation and hedge portfolio for any given barrier option. Market practitioners are often reluctant to quote on any barrier option given the potential valuation uncertainty and the hedging complexity. What we have shown is that this reluctance is not always justified—sometimes a barrier option is much less risky and easier to price than its European equivalent.

CHAPTER 10

Exotic Cliquets

The most obvious example of a forward-skew dependent claim is a cliquet. We already saw two examples of simple cliquet contracts in Chapter 8. As we noted there, a cliquet is a sequence of cliquettes, forward-starting options whose terms are set on the reset dates. The simplest and perhaps most common kind of cliquet is just a strip of forward-starting at-the-money European calls.

In this chapter, we look at some examples of exotic cliquet contracts. To make the discussion more concrete, we will take as our models three specific bonds issued by Mediobanca S.p.A.: a Locally Capped Globally Floored Cliquet, a Reverse Cliquet, and a Napoleon. It seems that Mediobanca has issued many different types of structured bond and the Mediobanca website (http://www.mediobanca.it) has a virtual treasure trove of well-written documents for the collector of exotic structures. Moreover, some of these deals have matured so that we can examine their ex post performance.

LOCALLY CAPPED GLOBALLY FLOORED CLIQUET

The "Mediobanca Bond Protection 2002–2005" (ISIN IT0003391353) has the Dow Jones EURO STOXX 50 index as underlying and offers guaranteed principal redemption plus an annual coupon payable on December 2 of each year given by

$$
\max\left[\left\{\sum_{t=1}^{12} \min\left(\max\left(r_t, -0.01\right), +0.01\right)\right\}, MinCoupon\right]
$$

where $MinCoupon = 0.02$ and each monthly return r_t is given by

$$
r_t = \frac{S_t - S_{t-1}}{S_{t-1}} - 1
$$

where S_t is the level of the EURO STOXX 50 index on the tth monthly reset date. The annual coupon is therefore capped at 12% and floored at 2%, hence the name *locally capped, globally floored cliquet* that is given to this type of structure.

According to the document, coupons are paid on December 2 of each year. The valuation dates t are the second day of each month except that the final valuation date for each coupon is November 25, one week before the coupon is paid.

If it weren't for the guaranteed minimum annual coupon, this particular Mediobanca deal would reduce to a simple strip of 1-month at-the-money call spreads (or equivalently put spreads according to taste). The minimum annual coupon acts as the global floor and each monthly return is capped at the local cap of 1%. Our intuition tells us that despite the global floor, this structure should behave as a strip of call spreads; adding a global floor is roughly equivalent to raising the lower strike of each spread. We would guess that the structure should be very sensitive to forward skew assumptions. Thus our prediction would be that a local volatility assumption would substantially underprice the deal because it generates forward skews that are too flat (the more negative the skew, the greater the value of a call spread).

Valuation under Heston and Local Volatility Assumptions

In order to get a sense for the dependency of the valuation of this cliquet on modeling assumptions, we may generate Monte Carlo paths under both Heston and local volatility assumptions with the parameters from Chapter 4.* Note that there is no suggestion that the Heston-Nandi parameters of Chapter 4 would have generated option prices remotely close to those obtaining on the issue date of the bond (December 2, 2002). All we are trying to do is to isolate the effect of modeling assumptions.

Figure 10.1 shows the value of this structure for different values of the minimum coupon (*MinCoupon* in the formula) in the Heston model with Heston-Nandi parameters:

$$\nu = 0.04; \ \bar{\nu} = 0.04; \ \lambda = 10; \ \eta = 1; \ \rho = -1$$

and under local volatility with the Heston local volatility approximation from Chapter 4:

$$\nu_{loc}(x_T, T) = \max\left[(\nu - \bar{\nu}')e^{-\lambda'T} + \bar{\nu}' - \eta\, x_T \left\{ \frac{1 - e^{-\lambda'T}}{\lambda'T} \right\}, 0 \right]$$

---

*Recall that these two sets of assumptions generate almost identical European option prices.

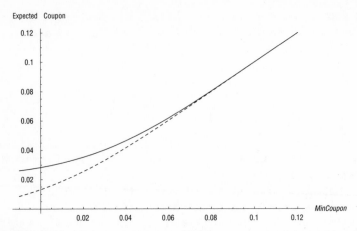

FIGURE 10.1 Value of the "Mediobanca Bond Protection 2002–2005" locally capped and globally floored cliquet (minus guaranteed redemption) as a function of *MinCoupon*. The solid line is stochastic volatility; the dashed line is local volatility.

with $\lambda' = \lambda + \eta/2$, $\bar{v}' = \bar{v}\lambda/\lambda'$. As usual, we assume zero interest rates and dividends.

We see that our intuition is justified. The actual structure has *minCoupon* = 2%; at that point, the expected coupon under Heston is 3.53% and the expected coupon under local volatility is only 2.55%, which corresponds to an upfront valuation difference of $3 \times 0.98 = 2.94\%$ with our usual assumption of zero rates and dividends. Relative to the profit of the provider of the exotic option component, 3.0% is a big number: It may well be more than his entire profit! The maximum coupon payable is 12% per year so the local volatility and Heston expected coupons must agree when *minCoupon* = 12% and from Figure 10.1, we see that they do. When *minCoupon* = −12% on the other hand, the structure is just a strip of European call spreads and the sensitivity to forward volatility skew (and so to the difference between Heston and local volatility assumptions) is maximized.

Performance

The historical performance of this bond is shown schematically in Figure 10.2.

The estimated historical bond coupons in Table 10.1 reflect the effective diversification that comes from averaging over 12 more-or-less independent capped and floored returns—they are rather close to the risk-free rate.* In

---

*Note that these are only estimates. The Calculation Agent always has the final say.

STOXX 50 Index

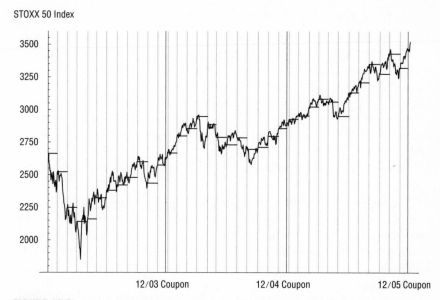

FIGURE 10.2 Historical performance of the "Mediobanca Bond Protection 2002–2005" locally capped and globally floored cliquet. The dashed vertical lines represent reset dates, the solid lines coupon setting dates and the solid horizontal lines represent fixings.

TABLE 10.1 Estimated "Mediobanca Bond Protection 2002–2005" coupons.

Fixing Date	Coupon
11/25/2003	3.91%
11/25/2004	3.55%
11/25/2005	4.14%

fact, the 3-year euro annual swap rate on the issue date (December 2, 2002) was 3.59%. It is pretty hard for an investor to make or lose much money in a structure like this.

REVERSE CLIQUET

The "Mediobanca 2000–2005 Reverse Cliquet Telecommunicazioni" (ISIN IT0001458600) has a basket of telecommunication stocks as underlying and offers guaranteed principal redemption plus a final premium P given by

$$P = \max \left[0, MaxCoupon + \sum_{i=1}^{10} \min [0, r_i] \right]$$

where each semi-annual return r_i is given by

$$r_i = \frac{basket_i - basket_{i-1}}{basket_i}$$

and $MaxCoupon = 100\%$.

We note that as in all such structures, principal is guaranteed but the coupons depend on the performance of some underlying index. In this case, there is no real periodic coupon. Instead (and this is also typical), a return is computed periodically and added to the final redemption amount. The maximum redemption amount achievable in this case is given by $Principal + MaxCoupon = 200\%$.

Without the guaranteed redemption feature, this Mediobanca structure would reduce to a simple strip of 6-month at-the-money puts; an investor would be short the strip of puts. The structure is termed a *reverse cliquet* because only negative returns contribute to the final payoff. It is therefore fair to assume that there would be very little skew dependence in the valuation. In fact, this is not typical and in general, each cliquette in a reverse cliquet has a local cap and local floor as in our previous example. The guaranteed redemption amount acts as a *global floor*.

Valuation under Heston and Local Volatility Assumptions

Figure 10.3 shows the value of this structure for different values of the maximum payoff (coupon in the formula) under Heston and local volatility assumptions with Heston-Nandi parameters exactly as before. We see that our intuition is justified. There is not a huge difference between a stochastic volatility and a local volatility valuation of the deal. With $MaxCoupon = 100\%$ as per the deal terms, the expected redemption amount is 43.9% in the Heston case and 42.0% in the local volatility case.

On closer examination, we note that the valuation of the deal is consistently higher under stochastic volatility than under local volatility. That's because although the investor is short at-the-money puts, he is also long the global floor which acts like a strip of out-of-the-money puts. This global floor is worth more under stochastic volatility than under local volatility reflecting the flatter forward volatility skews in a local volatility world.

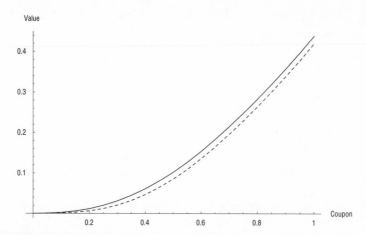

FIGURE 10.3 Value of the Mediobanca reverse cliquet (minus guaranteed redemption) as a function of *MaxCoupon*. The solid line is stochastic volatility; the dashed line is local volatility.

Performance

The historical performance of this bond is shown schematically in Figure 10.4. The extra data included prior to issuance of the deal in 2000 is to provide historical context. We see that as of the issue date, global telecommunications stocks had dropped substantially from their peak reached earlier in the year. One can imagine that the average investor might not have predicted that the basket of telecom stocks would have dropped a further 70% from inception to today, an 83% drop at the worst point. The investor would have been better off heeding the trader adage: "don't try to catch a falling knife."

Although at maturity the deal paid no more than the guaranteed principal, this is very substantially more than the investor would have got if he had held on to the underlying basket of telecommunications stocks. Moreover, the deal did have substantial upside unlike the capped and floored cliquet that we examined earlier. Again, for reference the euro 5-year annual swap rate was 5.73% on the issue date of May 18, 2000.

NAPOLEON

The payoff of the "Mediobanca 2002–2005 World Indices Euro Note Serie 46" (ISIN IT0003487524) again has guaranteed principal and pays an annual coupon given by

$$coupon_i = \max\left[0, MaxCoupon + \tilde{r}_i\right]$$

Basket index

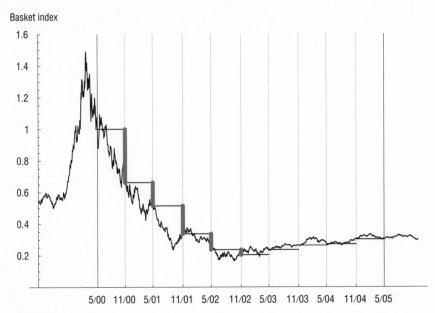

FIGURE 10.4 Historical performance of the "Mediobanca 2000–2005 Reverse Cliquet Telecommunicazioni" reverse cliquet. The vertical lines represent reset dates, the solid horizontal lines represent fixings and the vertical grey bars represent negative contributions to the cliquet payoff.

where $\tilde{r}_i$ is the average of the worst (most negative) monthly returns of three global stock indices—SPX, EURO STOXX 50, and NIKKEI 225 and *MaxCoupon* = 10%. Specifically,

$$\tilde{r}_i := \inf_{t_{i-1} < t_j < t_i} r_j.$$

Each cliquette has extreme dependence on the skew at the time the strike is set so the whole structure is extremely dependent on forward skew. The more negative the volatility skew, the greater the value of downside puts reflecting in turn the greater expected magnitude of downside moves and the lower the value of the structure. Our previous intuition would therefore lead us to predict that the Napoleon should be worth substantially less under stochastic volatility (with more negative returns on average) than under local volatility.

Valuation under Heston and Local Volatility Assumptions

Figure 10.5 shows the risk-neutral expected value of the Napoleon coupon for different values of the maximum annual coupon (MaxCoupon in the

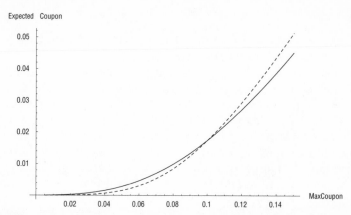

FIGURE 10.5 Value of (risk-neutral) expected Napoleon coupon as a function of *MaxCoupon*. The solid line is stochastic volatility; the dashed line is local volatility.

formula) computed as usual under Heston and local volatility assumptions with Heston-Nandi parameters from Chapter 4. As before, we assume zero interest rates and dividends.

This time, our previous intuition fails! Depending on the value of *MaxCoupon* the Heston Napoleon valuation can be higher or lower than the local volatility valuation. With *MaxCoupon* = 10% as in the deal terms, the expected Napoleon coupon is almost identical under the two sets of assumptions: 1.74% in each case.

The Napoleon-expected coupon is high at low volatility and low at high volatility with a lot of volatility convexity. Volatility convexity is underpriced in the local volatility model relative to stochastic volatility and in this case, the underpricing of volatility convexity may be the dominant effect. The Napoleon structure also has the feature that as the underlying falls, the expected coupon decreases and vega decreases—if the current return is negative enough for the coupon floor to be hit, future volatility can have no further effect. Maybe this cross-effect is more highly priced in the stochastic volatility model than in the local volatility model?

The moral of the story is clear: Intuition is well and good when the structure is familiar and well understood. But if a structure is either unfamiliar or not well understood, one should always look at the sensitivity of pricing to modeling assumptions as we have just done here. It's not enough to just compute sensitivity to model parameters within a given modeling framework: modeling assumptions themselves must be stressed.

Performance

The historical performance of the EURO STOXX 50 component of this Napoleon bond is shown schematically in Figure 10.6.

Referring to Table 10.2, we see that the estimated bond coupons are actually rather close to the risk-free rate, 3-year euro annual swap rate of 3.26% as of the issue date (December 20, 2002). Although the Napoleon structure appears to offer the investor the possibility of a very high coupon, the investor would have to be very lucky not to have one large negative monthly return out of twelve during a given coupon period. On the other hand, we shouldn't forget that principal is guaranteed; all of these complex cliquet structures are basically conservative for the investor.

Investor Motivation

The reader might wonder what it is that motivates an investor to consider one of these exotic cliquet structures. Cliquet deals were and continue to be targeted at European retail investors who were accustomed to investing in high-yielding government bonds. Of course, with the advent of the

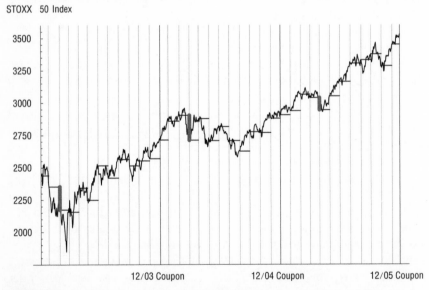

FIGURE 10.6 Historical performance of the STOXX 50 component of the "Mediobanca 2002–2005 World Indices Euro Note Serie 46" Napoleon. The light vertical lines represent reset dates, the heavy vertical lines coupon setting dates, the solid horizontal lines represent fixings and the thick grey bars represent the minimum monthly return of each coupon period.

TABLE 10.2 Worst monthly returns and estimated Napoleon coupons. Recall that the coupon is computed as 10% plus the worst monthly return averaged over the three underlying indices.

Date	$\tilde{r}_{STOXX50}$	$\tilde{r}_{SPX}$	$\tilde{r}_{NIKKEI225}$	Est. Coupon
12/20/2003	−7.61%	−5.69%	−11.61%	1.70%
12/20/2004	−6.62%	−4.26%	−9.12%	3.33%
12/20/2005	−3.09%	−3.91%	−6.36%	5.55%

euro and the global decline in yields, government bonds are no longer high yielding. One can surmise that these essentially conservative principal-guaranteed deals offer these investors the same security as a bond with the possibility of a high coupon. Although these structures are complex from the valuation and hedging perspective, they are not so hard to explain to a retail investor.

More on Napoleons

Although cliquet bonds are in general conservative deals for investors, they can be very hard to manage for the ultimate hedgers of the exotic option component. In the cases of locally capped globally floored and reverse cliquets, at least the hedger can roughly visualize what the structure is in terms of strips of forward-starting options. On the other hand, there doesn't seem to be any such neat (even approximate) decomposition of a Napoleon into conventional options.

In fact, exotic option traders at the time (2002 to 2003) that the Napoleon structure was popular were smart enough to realize that local volatility models were inappropriate because, as we keep noting, forward skews are too flat. However, the most common valuation technique wasn't stochastic volatility—it was the so-called independent increment technique. While to avoid arbitrage, returns must be uncorrelated, this technique effectively assumes that returns are independent of each other—even squared returns! Forward skews are roughly correct because 1-month returns are drawn (in Monte Carlo for example) from the 1-month risk-neutral distribution. However, forward volatility levels are deterministic and volatility convexity is underpriced.

It follows that the independent increment technique substantially underprices the Napoleon and since the lowest price invariably gets the deal, it was precisely those traders that were using the wrong model that got the business. Ironically, had those exotic traders used local volatility assumptions to price Napoleons, they would have lost less money. The importance of trying out different modeling assumptions cannot be overemphasized. Intuition is always fallible!

In a February 2004 *RISK* magazine article, Jeffery (2004) describes the situation well giving a sense of some of the pain suffered by exotic option traders.

CHAPTER 11

Volatility Derivatives

In this final chapter, we will investigate the pricing and hedging of claims that have realized volatility or variance (quadratic variation) as underlying. Although one might expect these recently developed instruments to be the most exotic and hard to price and hedge of all, it turns out that in some respects they are among the safest and easiest. Certainly some of the most elegant and robust constructions so far are to be found in this chapter.

SPANNING GENERALIZED EUROPEAN PAYOFFS

As usual, we assume that European options with all possible strikes and expirations are traded. In the spirit of the paper by Carr and Madan (1998), we now show that any twice-differentiable payoff at time T may be statically hedged using a portfolio of European options expiring at time T.

From Breeden and Litzenberger (1978), we know that we may write the *pdf* of the stock price S_T at time T as

$$p(S_T, T; S_t, t) = \left.\frac{\partial^2 \tilde{C}(S_t, K, t, T)}{\partial K^2}\right|_{K=S_T} = \left.\frac{\partial^2 \tilde{P}(S_t, K, t, T)}{\partial K^2}\right|_{K=S_T}$$

where $\tilde{C}$ and $\tilde{P}$ represent undiscounted call and put prices respectively.

Then the value of a claim with a generalized payoff $g(S_T)$ at time T is given by

$$\mathbb{E}\left[g(S_T)\,\middle|\, S_t\right] = \int_0^\infty dK\, p(K, T; S_t, t)\, g(K)$$

$$= \int_0^F dK\, \frac{\partial^2 \tilde{P}}{\partial K^2}\, g(K) + \int_F^\infty dK\, \frac{\partial^2 \tilde{C}}{\partial K^2}\, g(K)$$

where F represents the time-T forward price of the stock. Integrating by parts twice and using the put-call parity relation $\tilde{C}(K) - \tilde{P}(K) = F - K$ give

$$\mathbb{E}\left[g(S_T)\mid S_t\right] = \left.\frac{\partial \tilde{P}}{\partial K}\,g(K)\right|_0^F - \int_0^F dK\,\frac{\partial \tilde{P}}{\partial K}\,g'(K) + \left.\frac{\partial \tilde{C}}{\partial K}\,g(K)\right|_F^\infty$$

$$- \int_F^\infty dK\,\frac{\partial \tilde{C}}{\partial K}\,g'(K)$$

$$= g(F) - \int_0^F dK\,\frac{\partial \tilde{P}}{\partial K}\,g'(K) - \int_F^\infty dK\,\frac{\partial \tilde{C}}{\partial K}\,g'(K)$$

$$= g(F) - \left.\tilde{P}(K)g'(K)\right|_0^F + \int_0^F dK\,\tilde{P}(K)\,g''(K)$$

$$- \left.\tilde{C}(K)g'(K)\right|_F^\infty + \int_F^\infty dK\,\tilde{C}(K)\,g''(K)$$

$$= g(F) + \int_0^F dK\,\tilde{P}(K)\,g''(K) + \int_F^\infty dK\,\tilde{C}(K)\,g''(K) \qquad (11.1)$$

By letting $t \to T$ in equation (11.1), we see that any European-style twice-differentiable payoff may be replicated using a portfolio of European options with strikes from 0 to ∞ with the weight of each option equal to the second derivative of the payoff at the strike price of the option. This portfolio of European options is a static hedge because the weight of an option with a particular strike depends only on the strike price and the form of the payoff function and not on time or the level of the stock price. Note further that equation (11.1) is *completely model independent*.

Example: European Options

By using Dirac delta functions, we can extend the previous result to payoffs that are not twice-differentiable. Consider, for example, the portfolio of options required to hedge a single call option with payoff $(S_T - L)^+$. In this case $g''(K) = \delta(K - L)$ and equation (11.1) give

$$\mathbb{E}\left[(S_T - L)^+\right] = (F - L)^+ + \int_0^F dK\,\tilde{P}(K)\,\delta(K - L)$$

$$+ \int_F^\infty dK\,\tilde{C}(K)\,\delta(K - L)$$

$$= \begin{cases} (F - L) + \tilde{P}(L) & \text{if} \quad L < F \\ \tilde{C}(L) & \text{if} \quad L \geq F \end{cases}$$

$$= \tilde{C}(L)$$

with the last step following from put-call parity as before. In other words, the replicating portfolio for a European option is just the option itself.

Example: Amortizing Options

A useful variation on the payoff of the standard European option is given by the amortizing option with strike L with payoff

$$g(S_T) = \frac{(S_T - L)^+}{S_T}$$

Such options look particularly attractive when the volatility of the underlying stock is very high and the price of a standard European option is prohibitive. The payoff is effectively that of a European option whose notional amount declines as the option goes in-the-money. Then

$$g''(K) = \left\{ -\frac{2L}{S_T^3} \, \theta(S_T - L) + \frac{\delta(S_T - L)}{S_T} \right\} \Bigg|_{S_T = K}$$

Without loss of generality (but to make things easier), suppose $L > F$. Then substituting into equation (11.1) gives

$$\mathbb{E}\left[\frac{(S_T - L)^+}{S_T} \right] = \int_F^\infty dK \, \tilde{C}(K) \, g''(K)$$

$$= \frac{\tilde{C}(L)}{L} - 2L \int_L^\infty \frac{dK}{K^3} \, \tilde{C}(K)$$

and we see that an amortizing call option struck at L is equivalent to a European call option struck at L minus an infinite strip of European call options with strikes from L to ∞.

The Log Contract

Now consider a contract whose payoff at time T is $\log(S_T/F)$. Then $g''(K) = -1/S_T^2 \big|_{S_T = K}$ and it follows from equation (11.1) that

$$\mathbb{E}\left[\log\left(\frac{S_T}{F} \right) \right] = -\int_0^F \frac{dK}{K^2} \, \tilde{P}(K) - \int_F^\infty \frac{dK}{K^2} \, \tilde{C}(K)$$

Rewriting this equation in terms of the log-strike variable $k := \log(K/F)$, we get the promising-looking expression

$$\mathbb{E}\left[\log\left(\frac{S_T}{F}\right)\right] = -\int_{-\infty}^{0} dk\, p(k) - \int_{0}^{\infty} dk\, c(k) \qquad (11.2)$$

with

$$c(y) := \frac{\tilde{C}(Fe^y)}{Fe^y}; \; p(y) := \frac{\tilde{P}(Fe^y)}{Fe^y}$$

representing option prices expressed in terms of percentage of the strike price.

VARIANCE AND VOLATILITY SWAPS

We now revert to our usual assumption of zero interest rates and dividends. In this case, $F = S_0$ and applying Itô's lemma path by path

$$\log\left(\frac{S_T}{F}\right) = \log\left(\frac{S_T}{S_0}\right)$$

$$= \int_{0}^{T} d\log(S_t)$$

$$= \int_{0}^{T} \frac{dS_t}{S_t} - \int_{0}^{T} \frac{\sigma_{S_t}^2}{2} dt \qquad (11.3)$$

The second term on the rhs of equation (11.3) is immediately recognizable as half the total variance (or quadratic variation) $W_T := \langle x \rangle_T$ over the period $\{0, T\}$. The first term on the rhs represents the payoff of a hedging strategy which involves maintaining a constant dollar amount in stock (if the stock price increases, sell stock; if the stock price decreases, buy stock so as to maintain a constant dollar value of stock). Since the log payoff on the lhs can be hedged using a portfolio of European options as noted earlier, it follows that the total variance W_T may be replicated in a completely model-independent way so long as the stock price process is a diffusion. In particular, volatility may be stochastic or deterministic and equation (11.3) still applies.

Now taking the risk-neutral expectation of (11.3) and comparing with equation (11.2), we obtain

$$\mathbb{E}\left[\int_0^T \sigma_{S_t}^2 dt\right] = -2\,\mathbb{E}\left[\log\left(\frac{S_T}{F}\right)\right]$$

$$= 2\left\{\int_{-\infty}^0 dk\,p(k) + \int_0^\infty dk\,c(k)\right\} \qquad (11.4)$$

We see explicitly that, as originally noted by Dupire (1992) and then by Derman, Kamal, Kani, and Zou (1996), the fair value of total variance is given by the value of an infinite strip of European options in a completely *model independent* way so long as the underlying process is a diffusion.

Variance Swaps

Although trading in variance and volatility swaps really only began in the late 1990s, there is already a significant literature describing these contracts and the practicalities of hedging them including articles by Chriss and Morokoff (1999) and Demeterfi, Derman, Kamal, and Zou (1999).

In fact, a variance swap is not really a swap at all but a forward contract on the realized annualized variance. The payoff at time T is

$$N \times A \times \left\{\frac{1}{N}\sum_{i=1}^N \left\{\log\left(\frac{S_i}{S_{i-1}}\right)\right\}^2 - \left\{\frac{1}{N}\log\left(\frac{S_N}{S_0}\right)\right\}^2\right\} - N \times K_{var}$$

where N is the notional amount of the swap, A is the annualization factor and K_{var} is the strike price. Annualized variance may or may not be defined as mean-adjusted in practice so the corresponding drift term in the above payoff may or may not appear.

From a theoretical perspective, the beauty of a variance swap is that it may be replicated perfectly assuming a diffusion process for the stock price as shown in the previous section. From a practical perspective, market operators may express views on volatility using variance swaps without having to delta hedge.

Variance swaps took off as a product in the aftermath of the LTCM meltdown in late 1998 when implied stock index volatility levels rose to unprecedented levels. Hedge funds took advantage of this by paying variance in swaps (selling the realized volatility at high implied levels). The key to their willingness to pay on a variance swap rather than sell options was that a variance swap is a pure play on realized volatility—no labor-intensive delta hedging or other path dependency is involved. Dealers were happy to buy vega at these high levels because they were structurally short vega (in the aggregate) through sales of guaranteed equity-linked investments to retail investors and were getting badly hurt by high implied volatility levels.

Variance Swaps in the Heston Model

Recall that in the Heston model, instantaneous variance v follows the process:

$$dv(t) = -\lambda(v_t - \bar{v})dt + \eta \sqrt{v_t}\,dZ$$

It follows that the expectation of the total variance W_T is given by

$$\mathbb{E}\,[W_T] = \mathbb{E}\left[\int_0^T v_t\,dt\right]$$

$$= \int_0^T \hat{v}_t\,dt$$

$$= \frac{1 - e^{-\lambda T}}{\lambda}\,(v - \bar{v}) + \bar{v}T$$

The expected annualized variance is given by

$$\frac{1}{T}\mathbb{E}\,[W_T] = \frac{1 - e^{-\lambda T}}{\lambda T}\,(v - \bar{v}) + \bar{v}$$

We see that the expected variance in the Heston model depends only on v, $\bar{v}$ and λ. It does not depend on the volatility of volatility η. Since the value of a variance swap depends only on the prices of European options, it cannot depend on the specific dynamics assumed (local or stochastic volatility, for example).

Dependence on Skew and Curvature

We know that the implied volatility of an at-the-money forward option in the Heston model is lower than the square root of the expected variance (just think of the shape of the implied distribution of the final stock price in Heston). In practice, we start with a strip of European options of a given expiration and we would like to know how we should expect the price of a variance swap to relate to the at-the-money-forward implied volatility, the volatility skew and the volatility curvature (smile).

It turns out that there is a very elegant exact expression for the fair value of variance. Define

$$z(k) = d_2 = -\frac{k}{\sigma_{BS}(k)\sqrt{T}} - \frac{\sigma_{BS}(k)\sqrt{T}}{2}$$

Intuitively, z measures the log-moneyness of an option in implied standard deviations. Then

$$\mathbb{E}[W_T] = \int_{-\infty}^{\infty} dz\, N'(z)\, \sigma_{BS}^2(z)T \qquad (11.5)$$

To see this formula is plausible, it is obviously correct when there is no volatility skew. We now proceed to prove it.

Proof of Equation (11.5)* As usual, the undiscounted European call option price is given by

$$C = F\left\{ N\left(-\frac{k}{\sqrt{w}} + \frac{\sqrt{w}}{2}\right) - e^k N\left(-\frac{k}{\sqrt{w}} - \frac{\sqrt{w}}{2}\right) \right\}$$

where $k := \log(K/F)$ is the log-strike.

Differentiating wrt the strike K we obtain

$$\frac{\partial C}{\partial K} = \frac{1}{K}\frac{\partial C}{\partial k} = -N\left(-\frac{k}{\sqrt{w}} - \frac{\sqrt{w}}{2}\right) + N'\left(-\frac{k}{\sqrt{w}} - \frac{\sqrt{w}}{2}\right)\frac{\partial \sqrt{w}}{\partial k}$$

Then with the notation

$$d_1 = -\frac{k}{\sqrt{w}} + \frac{\sqrt{w}}{2}; \; d_2 = -\frac{k}{\sqrt{w}} - \frac{\sqrt{w}}{2}$$

and differentiating again wrt K, we obtain

$$
\begin{aligned}
\frac{\partial^2 C}{\partial K^2} &= \frac{1}{K}\frac{\partial}{\partial k}\left\{ -N\left(-\frac{k}{\sqrt{w}} - \frac{\sqrt{w}}{2}\right) + N'\left(-\frac{k}{\sqrt{w}} - \frac{\sqrt{w}}{2}\right)\frac{\partial \sqrt{w}}{\partial k} \right\} \\
&= \frac{N'(d_2)}{K}\left\{ -\frac{\partial d_2}{\partial k}\left(1 + d_2\frac{\partial \sqrt{w}}{\partial k}\right) + \frac{\partial^2 \sqrt{w}}{\partial k^2} \right\} \\
&= \frac{N'(d_2)}{K}\left\{ \frac{1}{\sqrt{w}}\left(d_1 d_2\left(\frac{\partial \sqrt{w}}{\partial k}\right)^2 - \frac{2k}{\sqrt{w}}\frac{\partial \sqrt{w}}{\partial k} + 1\right) + \frac{\partial^2 \sqrt{w}}{\partial k^2} \right\}
\end{aligned}
$$

---

*This particularly neat proof is due to Chiyan Luo.

As discussed earlier, the fair value of a variance swap under diffusion may be obtained by valuing a contract that pays $2 \log(S_T/F)$ at maturity T. Brute-force calculation leads to

$$2\mathbb{E}\left[\log\frac{S_T}{F}\right] = 2\int_0^\infty dK \log\left(\frac{K}{F}\right)\frac{\partial^2 C}{\partial K^2}$$

$$= 2\int_{-\infty}^\infty dk\, k\, N'(d_2)\left\{-\frac{\partial d_2}{\partial k}\left(1 + d_2\frac{\partial\sqrt{w}}{\partial k}\right) + \frac{\partial^2\sqrt{w}}{\partial k^2}\right\}$$

$$= 2\int_{-\infty}^\infty dk\, N'(d_2)\left\{-k\frac{\partial d_2}{\partial k} - \frac{\partial\sqrt{w}}{\partial k}\right\}$$

$$= \int_{-\infty}^\infty dk\, N'(d_2)\frac{\partial d_2}{\partial k}\, w$$

which recovers equation (11.5) as required.   □

Now consider the following simple parameterization of the BS implied variance skew:

$$\sigma_{BS}^2(z) = \sigma_0^2 + \alpha\, z + \beta\, z^2$$

Substituting into equation (11.5) and integrating, we obtain

$$\mathbb{E}[W_T] = \sigma_0^2 T + \beta T$$

We see that skew makes no contribution to this expression, only the curvature contributes. The intuition for this is simply that increasing the skew does not change the average level of volatility, but increasing the curvature β increases the prices of puts and calls in equation (11.2) and always increases the fair value of variance.

The Effect of Jumps

Let x_t denote the return of a compound Poisson process so that

$$x_T = \sum_i^{N_T} y_i$$

with the y_i *iid* and N_T a Poisson process with mean $\lambda\, T$. Define the quadratic variation as

$$\langle x\rangle_T = \sum_i^{N_T} |y_i|^2$$

Then

$$\mathbb{E}\left[\langle x \rangle_T\right] = \mathbb{E}\left[N_T\right] \mathbb{E}\left[|y_i|^2\right] = \lambda\, T \int_0^\infty y^2\, \mu(y)\, dy$$

Also

$$\mathbb{E}\left[x_T\right] = \lambda\, T \int_0^\infty y\, \mu(y)\, dy$$

and

$$\mathbb{E}\left[x_T^{\,2}\right] = \lambda\, T \int_0^\infty y^2\, \mu(y)\, dy + (\lambda\, T)^2 \left(\int_0^\infty y\, \mu(y)\, dy\right)^2$$

So

$$\mathbb{E}\left[\langle x \rangle_T\right] = \mathbb{E}\left[x_T^{\,2}\right] - \mathbb{E}\left[x_T\right]^2 = \mathrm{Var}\left[x_T\right]$$

That is, expected quadratic variation is just the variance of the terminal distribution for compound Poisson processes! We know this result is correct for Black-Scholes with constant volatility, but obviously it's not true in general (for example in the Heston model).

We can express the first two moments of the final distribution in terms of strips of European options using equation (11.1) as follows:

$$\mathbb{E}\left[x_T\right] = \mathbb{E}\left[\log(S_T/F)\right] = -\int_{-\infty}^0 dk\, p(k) - \int_0^\infty dk\, c(k)$$

$$\mathbb{E}\left[x_T^{\,2}\right] = \mathbb{E}\left[\log^2(S_T/F)\right] = -\int_{-\infty}^0 dk\, 2\, k\, p(k) - \int_0^\infty dk\, 2\, k\, c(k)$$

So, for a compound Poisson process, if we know European option prices, we may compute expected quadratic variation (i.e., compute the value of a variance swap) by computing the variance of the terminal distribution.

On the other hand, if the underlying process is a diffusion, we may compute expected quadratic variation using equation (11.4) in terms of the log-strip

$$\mathbb{E}\left[\langle x \rangle_T\right] = -2\, \mathbb{E}\left[x_T\right] = 2 \left\{\int_{-\infty}^0 dk\, p(k) + \int_0^\infty dk\, c(k)\right\}$$

So, if the underlying process is compound Poisson, we have one way of computing $\mathbb{E}\left[\langle x \rangle_T\right]$ and if the underlying process is a diffusion we have another. In reality, we're not sure what the underlying process is so we would like to know how much difference the choice of underlying process makes.

To compute this, we first note that from the definition of characteristic function,

$$\mathbb{E}\left[\log\left(S_T/F\right)\right] = -i\,\frac{\partial}{\partial u}\phi_T(u)\bigg|_{u=0}$$

Also note that if jumps are independent of the continuous process as they are in both the Merton and SVJ models, the characteristic function may be written as the product of a continuous part and a jump part

$$\phi_T(u) = \phi_T^C(u)\,\phi_T^J(u)$$

where the superscripts C and J refer to the continuous and jump parts respectively. From the Lévy-Khintchine representation of Chapter 5,

$$-i\,\frac{\partial}{\partial u}\,\phi_T^J(u)\bigg|_{u=0} = \lambda\,T\int_0^T \left(1+y-e^y\right)\mu(y)\,dy$$

On the other hand, we already showed above that

$$\mathbb{E}\left[\langle x^J\rangle_T\right] = \lambda\,T\int_0^T y^2\,\mu(y)\,dy$$

It follows that the difference between the fair value of a variance swap and the value of the log-strip is given by

$$\mathbb{E}\left[\langle x\rangle_T\right] + 2\,\mathbb{E}\left[x_T\right] = 2\,\lambda\,T\int_0^T \left(1+y+y^2/2-e^y\right)\mu(y)\,dy$$

Noting that the expression $1+y+y^2/2$ is just the first three terms in the Taylor expansion of e^y, we conclude that the error introduced by valuing a variance swap using the log-strip of equation (11.4) is of the order of the jump-size cubed. If there are no jumps of course, the log-strip values the variance swap correctly.

Example: Lognormally Distributed Jumps with Mean α and Standard Deviation δ In this case

$$\mathbb{E}\left[\langle x \rangle_T\right] + 2\,\mathbb{E}\left[x_T\right] = \lambda T\left(\alpha^2 + \delta^2\right) + 2\lambda T\left(1 + \alpha - e^{\alpha + \delta^2/2}\right)$$

$$= -\frac{1}{3}\lambda T\alpha\left(\alpha^2 + 3\delta^2\right) + \text{higher order terms}$$

Putting $\alpha = -0.09$, $\delta = 0.14$ and $\lambda = 0.61$, from Bakshi, Cao, and Chen (1997), we get an error of only 0.00122427 per year on a 1-year variance swap, which at 20% volatility corresponds to 0.30% in volatility terms.

Volatility Swaps

Realized volatility Σ_T is the square root of realized variance $V_T := \langle x \rangle_T / T$ and we know that the expectation of the square root of a random variable is less than (or equal to) the square root of the expectation. The difference between $\sqrt{V_T}$ and Σ_T is known as the *convexity adjustment*.

Figure 11.1 shows how the payoff of a variance swap compares with the payoff of a volatility swap.

Intuitively the magnitude of the convexity adjustment must depend on the volatility of realized volatility. Note that volatility does not have to be stochastic for realized volatility to be volatile; realized volatility Σ_T varies according to the path of the stock price even in a local volatility model.

In general, there is no replicating portfolio for a volatility swap and the magnitude of the convexity adjustment is model dependent. We will now compute the convexity adjustment in the Heston model.

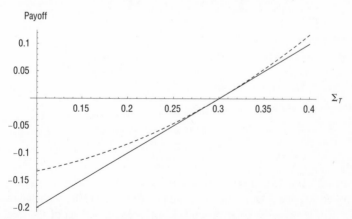

FIGURE 11.1   Payoff of a variance swap (dashed line) and volatility swap (solid line) as a function of realized volatility Σ_T. Both swaps are struck at 30% volatility.

Convexity Adjustment in the Heston Model

To proceed, we use the following trick:

$$\mathbb{E}\left[\sqrt{W_T}\right] = \frac{1}{2\sqrt{\pi}} \int_0^\infty \frac{1 - \mathbb{E}\left[e^{-\psi W_T}\right]}{\psi^{3/2}} \, d\psi \qquad (11.6)$$

We recognize that

$$\mathbb{E}\left[e^{-\psi W_T}\right] = \mathbb{E}\left[\exp\left\{-\psi \int_0^T v_t \, dt\right\}\right]$$

is formally identical to the expression for the value of a bond in the CIR model. Then from Cox, Ingersoll, and Ross (1985), we find that the Laplace transform of the total variance $W_T = \int_0^T v_t \, dt$ is given by

$$\mathbb{E}\left[e^{-\psi W_T}\right] = A \, e^{-\psi v B}$$

where

$$A = \left\{ \frac{2\phi \, e^{(\phi+\lambda)T/2}}{(\phi+\lambda)(e^{\phi T} - 1) + 2\phi} \right\}^{2\lambda\bar{v}/\eta^2}$$

$$B = \frac{2\,(e^{\phi T} - 1)}{(\phi+\lambda)(e^{\phi T} - 1) + 2\phi}$$

with $\phi = \sqrt{\lambda^2 + 2\psi\eta^2}$.

With some tedious algebra, we may verify that

$$\mathbb{E}\left[W_T\right] = -\frac{\partial}{\partial\psi} \mathbb{E}\left[e^{-\psi W_T}\right]\bigg|_{\psi=0}$$

$$= \frac{1 - e^{-\lambda T}}{\lambda}\,(v - \bar{v}) + \bar{v}T$$

as we found earlier by direct integration of the Heston SDE.

Computing the integral in equation (11.6) numerically using the Heston-Nandi parameters ($v = 0.04, \bar{v} = 0.04, \lambda = 10.0, \eta = 1.0$) of Chapter 4, we get the graph of the convexity adjustment as a function of time to expiration shown in Figure 11.2.

Convexity Adjustment

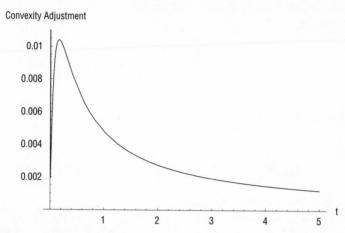

FIGURE 11.2 Annualized Heston convexity adjustment as a function of T with Heston-Nandi parameters.

Convexity Adjustment

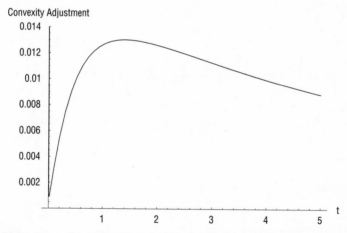

FIGURE 11.3 Annualized Heston convexity adjustment as a function of T with Bakshi, Cao, and Chen parameters.

Using Bakshi, Cao and Chen (1997) parameters ($v = 0.04, \bar{v} = 0.04, \lambda = 1.15, \eta = 0.39$), we get the graph of the convexity adjustment as a function of time to expiration shown in Figure 11.3.

To get intuition for what is going on here, compute the limit of the variance of V_T as $T \to \infty$ with $v = \bar{v}$ using

$$\mathrm{var}\,[W_T] = \mathbb{E}\left[W_T{}^2\right] - \{\mathbb{E}\,[W_T]\}^2$$

$$= \frac{\partial^2}{\partial\psi^2}\mathbb{E}\left[e^{-\psi\,W_T}\right]\Bigg|_{\psi=0} - \left\{\frac{\partial}{\partial\psi}\mathbb{E}\left[e^{-\psi\,W_T}\right]\Bigg|_{\psi=0}\right\}^2$$

$$= \bar{v}T\frac{\eta^2}{\lambda^2} + O(T^0)$$

Then, as $T \to \infty$, the standard deviation of *annualized* variance has the leading order behavior $\sqrt{\bar{v}/T}\,\eta/\lambda$. The convexity adjustment should be of the order of the standard deviation of annualized volatility over the life of the contract. From the last result, we expect this to scale as η/λ. Comparing Bakshi, Cao and Chen (BCC) parameters with Heston-Nandi parameters, we deduce that the convexity adjustment should be roughly 3.39 times greater with BCC parameters and that's what we see in the graphs.

VALUING VOLATILITY DERIVATIVES

Suppose the underlying process is a diffusion and that there is zero correlation between moves in the underlying and moves in volatility. With these assumptions, Carr and Lee (2005) show that any volatility derivative whose payoff is a function of the quadratic variation $\langle x \rangle_T$ may in principle be valued in terms of European options with expiration T. Friz and Gatheral (2005) present a practical algorithm for doing this. We now proceed to follow their reasoning.

Fair Value of the Power Payoff

Recall from equation (11.1) that generalized payoffs may be spanned according to

$$\mathbb{E}\,[g(S_T)] = g(F) + \int_0^F dK\,\tilde{P}(K,T)\,g''(K)$$

$$+ \int_F^\infty dK\,\tilde{C}(K,T)\,g''(K) \tag{11.7}$$

where $\tilde{C}$ and $\tilde{P}$ represent undiscounted call and put prices respectively and F represents the time-T forward price of the stock. With the substitution

$g(S_T) = S_T^p$, we obtain the replicating portfolio for a power payoff:

$$\mathbb{E}\left[S_T^p\right] = F^p + p\,(p-1)\int_0^F dK\,\tilde{P}(K,T)\,K^{p-2}$$

$$+ p\,(p-1)\int_F^\infty dK\,\tilde{C}(K,T)\,K^{p-2}$$

Define the log-strike $k := \log(K/F)$. Then

$$\mathbb{E}\left[S_T^p\right] = F^p \left\{1 + p\,(p-1)\int_{-\infty}^0 dk\,\hat{p}(k)\,e^{p\,k}\right.$$

$$\left. + p\,(p-1)\int_0^\infty dk\,\hat{c}(k)\,e^{p\,k}\right\} \tag{11.8}$$

where $\hat{p}(k)$ and $\hat{c}(k)$ denote the prices of puts and calls respectively in terms of percentage of strike.

If there is zero correlation between moves in the underlying and volatility moves, put-call symmetry holds, so that $\hat{p}(k) = e^{-k}\hat{c}(-k)$. We can then rewrite equation (11.8) as

$$\mathbb{E}\left[S_T^p\right] = F^p \left\{1 + 2\,p\,(p-1)\int_0^\infty dk\,e^{k/2}\,\hat{c}(k)\,\cosh\,(p-1/2)\,k\right\}$$

The Laplace Transform of Quadratic Variation under Zero Correlation

Under their assumptions of diffusion and zero correlation between spot moves and volatility moves, Carr and Lee (2005) derive an expression for the Laplace transform (moment generating function) of the quadratic variation $W_T := \langle x\rangle_T$ in terms of the fair value (11.8) of the power payoff. Since we know the replicating strip for the power payoff, it follows that we know the replicating strip for quadratic variation.

Following Carr and Lee, note that conditional on a particular realization of the volatility process (volatility path), under their zero-correlation assumption, the log-stock price

$$x_T = \int_0^T \sigma_t\,dW_t - \frac{1}{2}\,\langle x\rangle_T$$

is normally distributed with mean $-\langle x\rangle_T/2$ and variance $\langle x\rangle_T$. It follows that

$$\mathbb{E}\left[e^{p\,x_T}\right] = \mathbb{E}\left[e^{(p^2/2 - p/2)\,\langle x\rangle_T}\right] =: \mathbb{E}\left[e^{\lambda\,\langle x\rangle_T}\right]$$

with $\lambda = p^2/2 - p/2$. Inverting this, we obtain the moment generating function as

$$\mathbb{E}\left[e^{\lambda \langle x \rangle_T}\right] = \mathbb{E}\left[e^{p(\lambda)x_T}\right]$$

with $p(\lambda) = 1/2 \pm \sqrt{1/4 + 2\lambda}$.

From equation (11.8), we then have that

$$\mathbb{E}\left[e^{\lambda \langle x \rangle_T}\right] = 1 + p(\lambda)\,(p(\lambda) - 1)\left\{\int_{-\infty}^{0} dk\,\hat{p}(k)\,e^{p(\lambda)\,k}\right.$$

$$\left. + \int_{0}^{\infty} dk\,\hat{c}(k)\,e^{p(\lambda)\,k}\right\} \tag{11.9}$$

or alternatively

$$\mathbb{E}\left[e^{\lambda \langle x \rangle_T}\right] = 1 + 2\,p(\lambda)\,(p(\lambda) - 1)\int_{0}^{\infty} dk\,e^{k/2}\,\hat{c}(k)\,\cosh\left(p(\lambda) - 1/2\right)k$$

Noting that $p(\lambda)\,(p(\lambda) - 1) = 2\,\lambda$, we may simplify further to obtain

$$\mathbb{E}\left[e^{\lambda \langle x \rangle_T}\right] = 1 + 4\lambda\int_{0}^{\infty} dk\,e^{k/2}\,\hat{c}(k)\,\cosh\left(p(\lambda) - 1/2\right)k \tag{11.10}$$

The fair value of an exponential quadratic-variation (realized volatility) payoff follows immediately from equation (11.10). By taking derivatives, the fair value of any positive integral power of quadratic variation also follows. As a check, consider the fair value of the first power of quadratic variation—expected realized total variance. We have

$$\mathbb{E}\left[\langle x \rangle_T\right] = \frac{\partial}{\partial \lambda}\,\mathbb{E}\left[e^{\lambda \langle x \rangle_T}\right]\bigg|_{\lambda=0}$$

$$= \frac{\partial}{\partial \lambda}\left\{1 + 4\lambda\int_{0}^{\infty} dk\,e^{k/2}\,\hat{c}(k)\,\cosh\left(p(\lambda) - 1/2\right)k\right\}\bigg|_{\lambda=0}$$

$$= 4\int_{0}^{\infty} dk\,e^{k/2}\,\hat{c}(k)\,\cosh\left(p(0) - 1/2\right)k$$

$$= 4\int_{0}^{\infty} dk\,e^{k/2}\,\hat{c}(k)\,\cosh k/2$$

$$= 2 \int_0^\infty dk \, \hat{c}(k) \left\{ 1 + e^k \right\}$$

$$= 2 \left\{ \int_0^\infty dk \, \hat{c}(k) + \int_{-\infty}^0 dk \, \hat{p}(k) \right\}$$

which agrees exactly with our earlier result (11.4).

In principle, since we have an explicit expression for the moment generating function (*mgf*) of realized variance, we know its entire terminal (time T) pseudo-probability distribution and we may compute the fair value of any European-style claim on realized variance—knowing only market prices of European options! Unfortunately, the analogue of the replicating option strip for variance swaps doesn't exist for generic volatility derivatives. Friz and Gatheral (2005) show that although it's easy to write down a formal expression, the weights of the options in the strip are undefined.

The Fair Value of Volatility under Zero Correlation

After the variance swap, the next simplest claim to analyze is the volatility swap. Friz and Gatheral (2005) show that under the zero-correlation assumption,

$$\mathbb{E}\left[\sqrt{\langle x \rangle_T} \right] = \sqrt{2\pi} \, \hat{c}(0) + \sqrt{\frac{2}{\pi}} \int_0^\infty dk \, e^{k/2} I_1 \left(\frac{k}{2} \right) \hat{c}(k) \qquad (11.11)$$

where $I_n(\cdot)$ represents a modified Bessel function of the first kind.

That the at-the-money option should have a delta-function weight should come as no surprise as we are already familiar with the extremely accurate approximation

$$\hat{c}(0) \approx \frac{\sigma_{BS} \sqrt{T}}{\sqrt{2\pi}} \qquad (11.12)$$

for at-the-money forward European options.

To see just how dominant the contribution of the at-the-money forward European option is, consider a 1-year flat volatility smile with $\sigma_{BS}(k, 1) = 0.2$, $\forall k$. The first term in (11.11) evaluates to 0.1997 and the continuous strip of options with Bessel function weights to 0.0003. The total must of course give 0.2, which is the fair value of volatility when the volatility smile is flat (no convexity adjustment).

The formula (11.11) was originally derived from direct integration. Peter Friz subsequently provided the following more enlightening derivation of the weights by imposing that in the flat-smile Black-Scholes case where $\sigma_{BS}(k) = \sigma \; \forall k$, the value of the volatility swap should equal the implied volatility σ.

Proof In the flat smile case (without loss of generality we choose $\tau = 1$), we may write

$$\int_0^\infty dk \left\{ \sqrt{\frac{\pi}{2}} \, F'(k/2) + \sqrt{2\pi} \, \delta(k) \right\} e^{k/2} c_{BS}(k; \sigma) = \sigma \qquad (11.13)$$

for some F to be found with $F(0) = 1$. From integration by parts, we find that

$$\int_0^\infty dk \left\{ \sqrt{\frac{\pi}{2}} \, F'(k/2) + \sqrt{2\pi} \, \delta(k) \right\} e^{k/2} c_{BS}(k; \sigma)$$

$$= -\sqrt{2\pi} \left\{ \int_0^\infty dk \, F(k/2) \frac{\partial}{\partial k} \left[e^{k/2} c_{BS}(k; \sigma) \right] \right\}$$

Then differentiating each side of (11.13) with respect to σ we obtain

$$-\sqrt{2\pi} \left\{ \int_0^\infty dk \, F(k/2) \frac{\partial}{\partial k} \left[e^{k/2} \frac{\partial}{\partial \sigma} c_{BS}(k; \sigma) \right] \right\} = 1 \qquad (11.14)$$

for *every* choice of σ. That is, the vega of the option strip must be 1 no matter what the implied volatility is.

By taking explicit derivatives of the Black-Scholes formula, recalling our definition $c_{BS}(k; \sigma) := \exp(-k) \, C_{BS}(k, \sigma)$, we obtain

$$\frac{\partial}{\partial k} \left[e^{k/2} \frac{\partial}{\partial \sigma} c_{BS}(k; \sigma) \right] = -\frac{1}{\sqrt{2\pi}} \frac{k}{\sigma^2} \exp\left(-\frac{k^2}{2\sigma^2} \right) e^{-\sigma^2/8}$$

With $v := \sigma^2$, substitution into (11.14) and rearranging give

$$\int_0^\infty dk \, F(k/2) \frac{k}{v} \exp\left(-\frac{k^2}{2v} \right) = e^{v/8}$$

Now expand $F(k)$ in powers of k as

$$F(k) = \sum_{m=0}^\infty \alpha_m k^m$$

and integrate term-by-term to obtain

$$\sum_{m=0}^{\infty} \alpha_m \left(\frac{v}{2}\right)^{m/2} \left(\frac{m}{2}\right)! = \sum_{n=0}^{\infty} \left(\frac{v}{8}\right)^n \frac{1}{n!}$$

Equating powers of v and solving for α_m leads to

$$F(k) = \sum_{m=0}^{\infty} \frac{(k^2/4)^m}{(m!)^2}.$$

which we recognize this as the Bessel function $I_0(k)$. Finally we recall that the option weights in the options strip (11.13) are given by $F'(k/2)$ and note that

$$I_1(k) = \partial_k I_0(k)$$

to complete the proof. □

Replication of Volatility Swaps Even though we can express the fair value of volatility as the value of a weighted strip of European options (in the zero correlation case), the volatility replication strategy differs fundamentally from the variance replication strategy. In the variance case, we trade a strip of options at inception and thereafter rebalance daily only in the underlying and then only to maintain a constant dollar amount of the underlying in the hedge portfolio. In contrast, in the volatility case we have to continuously maintain a position in the at-the-money option: Each day, we sell the entire position, which is no longer at-the-money, and buy a new one. Unlike the variance strategy, this strategy is clearly not practical—the option bid-offer would kill the hedger.

Despite the fact that the zero-correlation assumption is completely unrealistic, at least in equity markets, the Carr-Lee result is tantalizing. For example, we'd like to know how tightly the prices of European options (which are assumed to be known) constrain the fair value of a volatility derivative.

A Simple Lognormal Model

Assume that $\log\left(\sqrt{\langle x \rangle_T}\right)$ is normally distributed with mean μ and variance s^2. Then $\log(\langle x \rangle_T)$ is also normally distributed with mean 2μ and variance $4s^2$. Volatility and variance swap values are given by respectively

$$\mathbb{E}[\sqrt{\langle x \rangle_T}] = e^{\mu + s^2/2}; \quad \mathbb{E}[\langle x \rangle_T] = e^{2\mu + 2s^2}$$

Solving for μ and s^2 gives

$$s^2 = 2 \log \left(\frac{\sqrt{\mathbb{E}\left[\langle X \rangle_T\right]}}{\mathbb{E}\left[\sqrt{\langle X \rangle_T}\right]} \right) ; \quad \mu = \log \left(\frac{\mathbb{E}\left[\sqrt{\langle X \rangle_T}\right]^2}{\sqrt{\mathbb{E}\left[\langle X \rangle_T\right]}} \right)$$

and the convexity adjustment is given by

$$\sqrt{\mathbb{E}\left[\langle X \rangle_T\right]} - \mathbb{E}\left[\sqrt{\langle X \rangle_T}\right] = \left(e^{s^2/2} - 1 \right) \mathbb{E}\left[\sqrt{\langle X \rangle_T}\right]$$

Incidentally, this simple lognormal assumption seems very reasonable; the empirical distribution of implied volatility changes looks lognormal and as noted in Chapter 8, the dynamics of the volatility skew are consistent with approximately lognormal volatility dynamics.

It follows that calls on variance may be valued using a Black-Scholes style formula:

$$\mathbb{E}\left[\langle x \rangle_T - K\right]^+ = e^{2\mu + 2s^2} N(\tilde{d}_1) - K N(\tilde{d}_2) \tag{11.15}$$

with

$$\tilde{d}_1 = \frac{-\frac{1}{2}\log K + \mu + 2s^2}{s}$$

$$\tilde{d}_2 = \frac{-\frac{1}{2}\log K + \mu}{s}.$$

In this simple lognormal model, the variance and volatility swap values (or equivalently the variance swap value plus the convexity adjustment) are all that is required to fix the values of all options on variance. Moreover, at least for the major equity indexes, there is a tight market in variance swaps and a somewhat less liquid market in the convexity adjustment.

A Heston Example Suppose the true dynamics of the underlying were Heston (recall that lognormal volatility is a much more realistic assumption) with BCC parameters

$$\lambda = 1.15, \rho = 0, \sigma_0^2 = \overline{\sigma}^2 = 0.04, \eta = 0.39.$$

We showed earlier how to compute the value of a volatility swap in terms of the Heston parameters. We can also easily compute the values of calls on variance in terms of the Heston parameters. Given the values of the variance and the volatility swap, we can also apply equation (11.15) to value the same calls on variance. How big is the error from applying the simple variance call formula?

In Figure 11.4, we compare prices of variance calls obtained from the approximate formula with those obtained from a direct numerical integration using the closed-form Heston characteristic function of realized variance.

Obviously, the two approaches must agree at zero strike because then we have just a variance swap. It's not clear how big the valuation error really is away from zero strike. To get a better sense for the error, in Figure 11.5, we compare the density we get by inverting the Heston characteristic function numerically and the approximate lognormal density with mean 2μ and variance $4s^2$.

We see that agreement is pretty close. And if agreement is so close in the Heston case where we believe the dynamics to be unrealistic, how much better should the agreement be when the underlying volatility dynamics are lognormal (the more realistic case)?

We conclude that the values of T-maturity volatility derivatives are in practice tightly constrained by the prices of expiration-T European options. To make the argument even more explicit, we fit our preferred stochastic volatility model (lognormal let's say) to the prices of European options, we set the correlation ρ to zero (this does not affect the value of volatility derivatives), compute the value of the volatility swap using (11.11) and apply our lognormal variance call option formula (11.15), confident that

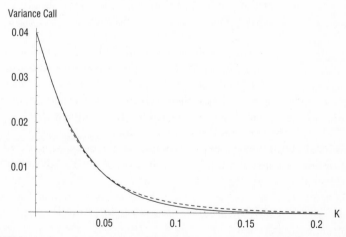

FIGURE 11.4 Value of 1-year variance call versus variance strike K with the BCC parameters. The solid line is a numerical Heston solution; the dashed line comes from our lognormal approximation.

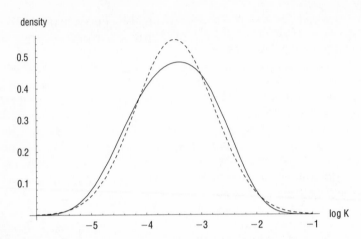

FIGURE 11.5 The pdf of the log of 1-year quadratic variation with BCC parameters. The solid line comes from an exact numerical Heston computation; the dashed line comes from our lognormal approximation.

the result will be robust to the specific parameters. The only constraint is that the fit to expiration-T European prices should be good.

Options on Volatility: More on Model Independence

We have argued so far that given the prices of European options of all strikes and expirations, the values of options on variance should be tightly constrained. The extent to which this is true and even how this claim should be precisely stated are as yet unresolved questions.

Elegant work by Bruno Dupire (Dupire 2005) shows how a mode-independent lower bound for calls on realized variance may be obtained by considering the delta hedging of a portfolio of European call options. The idea is to hedge in business time defined as the timescale of realized quadratic variation; the options are rehedged each time quadratic variation increases by a given amount. Unlike conventional delta hedging in (atomic) clock time, assuming no jumps, this hedging strategy guarantees profits on a short option position if realized volatility is below implied volatility (the volatility implied by the initial sale price). Conversely, the hedged option position is guaranteed to lose if realized volatility is higher than implied at inception. Losses are insured against by buying an option on quadratic variation. The hedger ends up short a portfolio of European options and long an option on realized variance with only positive payoffs. This portfolio must be worth at least zero, and a model-independent, lower bound on the price of an option on variance follows. In the same work, Dupire shows how solutions to the Skorokhod embedding problem can generate effective upper and lower bounds on the price of an option on variance constrained by known prices of European options.[*]

Returning to the lower bound, it has been conjectured[†] that the minimum possible value of an option on variance is the one generated from a local volatility model fitted to the volatility surface. Clearly options on variance have value even in a local volatility model because realized variance depends on the realized path of the stock price from inception to expiration. Given that local variance is a risk-neutral conditional expectation of instantaneous variance, it seems obvious that any other model would generate extra fluctuations of the local volatility surface relative to its initial state.

Between these model-independent upper and lower bounds, it seems reasonable to suppose that the fair value of an option on variance is closest to that given by a stochastic volatility model. We have spent much of this book arguing that local volatility models have unrealistic dynamics, so it's easy to reject the lower bound as representing fair value. On the other hand, the upper bound could represent some wild dynamics of the volatility surface. In practice, volatility surfaces are very well behaved. For example, Cont and da Fonseca (2002) do principal components analysis on time series of volatility surfaces and find that nearly all of the variance can be explained by three modes of fluctuation, which we may term volatility level, skew, and curvature. According to Cont and Fonseca, a staggering 94% of the variance of SPX volatility surface is explained by the first principal component which by inspection is roughly a change in level (i.e., a change in instantaneous volatility in our context).

Forde (2006) makes further progress by generalizing the Carr-Lee result to local-stochastic volatility models of the type

$$dS = \sigma(S)\sqrt{v}\,dZ$$

where $\sigma(S)$ is some deterministic function of S (a local volatility function) and v is stochastic but independent of Z. He shows how given a local volatility function $\sigma(S)$, the law of quadratic variation can be recovered from the smile at a single expiration by considering the prices of certain eigenfunction contracts. Such local stochastic volatility models are now standard in the foreign exchange markets where tight bid-ask spreads on claims such as one-touch options exclude plain stochastic volatility models. As mentioned earlier in Chapter 9, bid-ask spreads on one-touch equity options are not yet tight (to say the least) so the same pressure to add a

---

[*]Strictly speaking, the upper bound has only the status of a conjecture.
[†]It seems that Bruno Dupire is close to a formal proof.

local volatility component is not felt. In addition, the at-the-money volatility skew in equity markets is in general much more pronounced than in FX markets. This fact combined with empirical observations of volatility surface dynamics leads equity derivative modelers to generate skew from nonzero correlation between stock returns and volatility changes rather than from an explicit local volatility function.

LISTED QUADRATIC-VARIATION BASED SECURITIES

The VIX Index

In 2004, the CBOE listed futures on the VIX—an implied volatility index. Originally, the VIX computation was designed to mimic the implied volatility of an at-the-money 1-month option on the OEX index. It did this by averaging volatilities from eight options (puts and calls from the closest to ATM strikes in the nearest and next to nearest months). To facilitate trading in the VIX, the definition of the index was changed. Here is an excerpt from the FAQ section on the CBOE website:

> "How is VIX being changed? Three important changes are being made to update and improve VIX: 1. The New VIX is calculated using a wide range of strike prices in order to incorporate information from the volatility skew. The original VIX used only at-the-money options. 2. The New VIX uses a newly developed formula to derive expected volatility directly from the prices of a weighted strip of options. The original VIX extracted implied volatility from an option-pricing model. 3. The New VIX uses options on the S&P 500 Index, which is the primary U.S. stock market benchmark. The original VIX was based on S&P 100 Index (OEX) option prices.
>
> Why is the CBOE making changes to the VIX? CBOE is changing VIX to provide a more precise and robust measure of expected market volatility and to create a viable underlying index for tradable volatility products.
>
> The New VIX calculation reflects the way financial theorists, risk managers and volatility traders think about—and trade—volatility. As such, the New VIX calculation more closely conforms to industry practice than the original VIX methodology. It is simpler, yet it yields a more robust measure of expected volatility. The New VIX is more robust because it pools information from option prices over a wide range of strike prices thereby capturing the whole volatility skew, rather than just the volatility implied by

at-the-money options. The New VIX is simpler because it uses a formula that derives the market expectation of volatility directly from index option prices rather than an algorithm that involves backing implied volatilities out of an option-pricing model. The changes also increase the practical appeal of VIX. As noted previously, the New VIX is calculated using options on the S&P 500 index, the widely recognized benchmark for U.S. equities, and the reference point for the performance of many stock funds, with over $800 billion in indexed assets. In addition, the S&P 500 is the domestic index most often used in over-the-counter volatility trading. This powerful calculation supplies a script for replicating the New VIX with a static portfolio of S&P 500 options. This critical fact lays the foundation for tradable products based on the New VIX, critical because it facilitates hedging and arbitrage of VIX derivatives. CBOE has announced plans to list VIX futures and options in Q4 2003, pending regulatory approval. These will be the first of an entire family of volatility products.

This explanation is intriguing. To see what the CBOE means, consider the VIX definition (converted to our notation) as specified in the CBOE white paper (CBOE 2003):

$$VIX^2 = \frac{2}{T} \sum_i \frac{\Delta K_i}{K_i^2} Q_i(K_i) - \frac{1}{T} \left[\frac{F}{K_0} - 1 \right]^2 \qquad (11.16)$$

where Q_i is the price of the out-of-the-money option with strike K_i and K_0 is the highest strike below the forward price F.

We recognize the VIX formula (11.16) as a straightforward discretization of equation (11.4) making clear the reason why the CBOE implies that the new index permits replication of volatility.

To see this, we start with the log-strip formula (11.4) for valuing variance. Rewriting it in terms of strikes rather than log-strikes, and noting from CBOE (2003) that K_0 is defined to be the first strike below the index level F, we obtain (with obvious notation)

$$
\begin{aligned}
\frac{VIX^2 T}{2} &= \int_0^F \frac{dK}{K^2} P(K) + \int_F^\infty \frac{dK}{K^2} C(K) \\
&= \int_0^{K_0} \frac{dK}{K^2} P(K) + \int_{K_0}^\infty \frac{dK}{K^2} C(K) + \int_{K_0}^F \frac{dK}{K^2} (P(K) - C(K)) \\
&=: \int_0^\infty \frac{dK}{K^2} Q(K) + \int_{K_0}^F \frac{dK}{K^2} (K - F)
\end{aligned}
$$

$$\approx \int_0^\infty \frac{dK}{K^2} Q(K) + \frac{1}{K_0^2} \int_{K_0}^F dK\ (K - F)$$

$$= \int_0^\infty \frac{dK}{K^2} Q(K) - \frac{1}{K_0^2} \frac{(K_0 - F)^2}{2}$$

One possible discretization of this last expression is

$$VIX^2 = \frac{2}{T} \sum_i \frac{\Delta K_i}{K_i^2} Q_i(K_i) - \frac{1}{T} \left[\frac{F}{K_0} - 1 \right]^2$$

as in the VIX specification (11.16).

VXB Futures

Volume on VXB futures (the VXB index is defined to be 10 times the VIX) has been negligible. For example, as of December 8, 2004, the December VXB future had been trading an average of 155 contracts per day. At the then price of 132.30, that corresponds to roughly $2 million of notional per day. In contrast, Dec04 SPX futures were trading around 50,000 contracts corresponding to around $15 *billion* of notional per day.

As a practical indication of how the replicating strip (11.4) is associated with expected variance, settlement is on the Wednesday before the third Friday based on the opening prices of options expiring in the following month, the third Friday being the day on which the payoffs of SPX options are set.

A Subtlety   VXB futures settle based on the *square root* of the value of the replicating strip (i.e., on volatility rather than variance) so there must be a convexity adjustment. However, this isn't exactly the same as the convexity adjustment

$$\sqrt{\mathbb{E}[W_T]} - \mathbb{E}[\sqrt{W_T}]$$

that we computed earlier.

As of the valuation date, the convexity adjustment relevant to the VXB futures contract is given by

$$\sqrt{\mathbb{E}[W_{t,T}]} - \mathbb{E}\left[\sqrt{\mathbb{E}_t[W_{t,T}]} \right]$$

where t is the settlement date, T is the expiration date of options in the strip and the expectation is computed as of some valuation date prior to t.

As before, we can easily compute $\mathbb{E}[W_{t,T}]$ from strips of options expiring at times t and T respectively but we need a model to compute $\mathbb{E}\left[\sqrt{\mathbb{E}_t[W_{t,T}]}\right]$.

One obvious question is where the market prices this convexity adjustment. As of December 8, 2004, the spot VXB was at 132.30. Computing the expected forward variances $\mathbb{E}[W_{t,T}]$ from market prices of options we obtain the empirical convexity adjustments shown in Table 11.1.

The next question is what the VXB futures are worth theoretically.

VXB Convexity Adjustment in the Heston Model   To compute the VXB convexity adjustment in the Heston model, we first note that expected 1-month expected total variance $W_{t,T}$ given the instantaneous variance v_t is

$$f(v) = \mathbb{E}[W_{t,T}] = (v - \bar{v}) \frac{1 - e^{-\lambda \tau}}{\lambda} + \bar{v}\tau$$

with $\tau = T - t$.

Then

$$\mathbb{E}\left[\sqrt{W_{t,T}}\right] = \int_0^\infty q(v|v_0)\sqrt{f(v)}\,dv \qquad (11.17)$$

where $q(v|v_0)$ is the pdf of instantaneous variance v given the initial variance v_0.

Computing the integral in equation (11.17) numerically using Heston parameters from a fit to December 8, 2004, data, we get the graph of the convexity adjustment as a function of time to expiration shown in Figure 11.6.

We see that for the two futures maturities listed in Table 11.1, the Heston convexity adjustments were respectively around 7.4 and 8.6 points—not so different from the empirically observed numbers.

TABLE 11.1   Empirical VXB convexity adjustments as of December 8, 2004.

Expiry	VXB Price	Fwd Variance	Convexity Adjustment
Spot	132.30	132.30	0.00
Jan-05	144.20	149.09	4.89
Feb-05	153.30	159.63	6.33

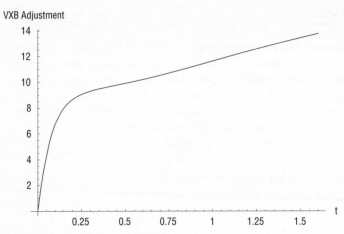

FIGURE 11.6 Annualized Heston VXB convexity adjustment as a function of t with Heston parameters from December 8, 2004, SPX fit.

Dupire's Method for Valuing VXB Futures Recall that roughly speaking, at maturity T_1, a VXB future pays

$$\mathbb{E}_{T_1}[\sqrt{\langle x \rangle_{T_1,T_2}}] =: Y$$

where $\langle x \rangle_{T_1,T_2} = \langle x \rangle_{T_2} - \langle x \rangle_{T_1}$ between times T_1 and T_2. Also, by definition,

$$\mathbb{E}_t[Y]^2 = \mathbb{E}_t[Y^2] - \mathrm{Var}_t[Y]$$

Dupire (2005) notes that the convexity adjustment is given precisely by the variance of VXB futures themselves. Since VXB futures trade, the variance $\mathrm{Var}_t[Y]$ may be estimated historically from the time series of futures prices.

The fair value of the VIX future is then given by

$$\mathbb{E}_t[Y] = \sqrt{\mathbb{E}_t[Y^2] - \mathrm{Var}_t[Y]}$$

Knock-on Benefits

Although VXB futures contracts haven't been very successful by usual futures standards, they have contributed to stimulating the OTC market to very substantially tighten spreads. Now SPX variance swaps can be traded from six months to five years with bid-offer spreads of as little as 0.5 vol. points. Single-stock variance swaps are also now actively quoted; for the top 50 U.S. single stock names, bid-offer spreads are around 2.5 vol. points at the time of writing.

SUMMARY

Although volatility derivatives are a relatively recent innovation, they are already widely traded, not least because from a practical perspective, valuation is well understood. We saw that although the standard variance swap valuation approach assumes diffusion, the existence of reasonably sized jumps wouldn't change the valuation by much. We also saw that although the relationship between the valuation of options on variance and European option prices is currently only partially understood, it's pretty clear from a practical perspective how to value them. From a theoretical perspective, there are surely further connections to be made between the valuation of volatility derivatives and the dynamics of the underlying process.

Postscript

Dear reader, having got this far, I hope that you have gained some useful insights into volatility surface modeling and applications of the resulting models. It should be apparent to you, not least from the list of references, that research in financial mathematics continues apace with more researchers getting involved each year.

This is no doubt part of a wider trend where mathematics is rapidly finding new applications in every facet of life from the hard sciences such as physics and biology to the softer sciences such as economics and sociology. What may be less obvious is that there is flow in the other direction, from applications to pure and applied mathematics. Financial applications often motivate new results in probability theory and stochastic analysis, just as the latest theories in physics often motivate new results in branches of pure mathematics such as topology and algebraic geometry. Obviously financial applications also motivate the invention of new or enhanced numerical computation schemes.

The moral of all this is that even though it may seem that everything in financial mathematics is reasonably well understood and that there is nothing much left to do, there is always more to do. What may be an adequate approximation for practical purposes today may not be tomorrow as market liquidity increases and bid-offer spreads continue their inexorable decline. A numerical scheme that may not be practical today may become so tomorrow as computing power increases. So I say to those readers who may hesitate to get involved because they feel they are too late, get involved, there's plenty more to do!

Bibliography

Albrecher, Hansjörg, Philipp Mayer, Wim Schoutens and Jurgen Tistaert, 2007, The Little Heston Trap, Wilmott Magazine 1, 73–82.

Alfonsi, Aurélien. 2005. On the discretization schemes for the CIR (and Bessel squared) processes. Discussion paper CERMICS, projet MATHFI, Ecole Nationale des Ponts et Chaussées Marne-la-vallée.

Andersen, Leif, and Jesper Andreasen. 2000. Jump-diffusion processes: Volatility smile fitting and numerical methods for option pricing. *Review of Derivatives Research* 4, 231–262.

———, and Rupert Brotherton-Ratcliffe. 2001. Extended LIBOR market models with stochastic volatility. Discussion paper Banc of America Securities and Gen Re Securities.

Avellaneda, Marco, C. Friedman, R. Holmes, and D. Samperi. 1997. Calibrating volatility surfaces via relative-entropy minimization. *Applied Mathematical Finance* 4, 37–64.

Avellaneda, Marco, A. Levy, and Antonio Parás. 1995. Pricing and hedging derivative securities in markets with uncertain volatilities. *Applied Mathematical Finance* 2, 73–88.

Bakshi, Gurdip, Charles Cao, and Zhiwu Chen. 1997. Empirical performance of alternative option pricing models. *The Journal of Finance* 52, 2003–2049.

Benaim, Shalom, and Peter Friz. 2006. Regular variation and smile asymptotics. Discussion paper Cambridge University, Department of Pure Mathematics and Mathematical Statistics.

Berestycki, Henri, Jérôme Busca, and Igor Florent. 2002. Asymptotics and calibration of local volatility models. *Quantitative Finance* 2, 61–69.

Black, F., and M. Scholes. 1973. The pricing of options and corporate liabilities. *Journal of Political Economy* 81, 631–659.

Brace, Alan, B. Goldys, F. Klebaner, and R. Womersley. 2001. Market model of stochastic volatility with applications to the BGM model. Discussion paper Department of Statistics, University of New South Wales.

Breeden, D., and R. Litzenberger. 1978. Prices of state-contingent claims implicit in option prices. *Journal of Business* 51, 621–651.

Brigo, Damiano, and Fabio Mercurio. 2003. Lognormal-mixture dynamics and calibration to market volatility smiles. *International Journal of Theoretical and Applied Finance* 5, 427–446.

Broadie, Mark, Paul Glasserman, and Steven G. Kou. 1999. On pricing of discrete barrier options. *Finance and Stochastics* 3, 55–82.

Broadie, Mark, and Özgür Kaya. 2004. Exact simulation of stochastic volatility and other affine jump diffusion processes. Discussion paper Columbia University, Graduate School of Business.

Carr, Peter, and Andrew Chou. 1997. Breaking barriers. *Risk* 10, 139–145.

————, and Roger W. Lee. 2005. Robust replication of volatility derivatives. Discussion paper Bloomberg LP and University of Chicago.

————, and Dilip Madan. 1998. Towards a theory of volatility trading. In Robert A. Jarrow, ed., *Volatility: New Estimation Techniques for Pricing Derivatives*, Chap. 29, pp. 417–427 (Risk Books).

————, and Dilip B. Madan. 1999. Option valuation using the fast Fourier transform. *The Journal of Computational Finance* 2, 61–73.

CBOE, 2003, VIX: CBOE volatility index, http://www.cboe.com/micro/vix/vixwhite.pdf.

Chriss, Neil, and William Morokoff. 1999. Market risk for variance swaps. *Risk* 12, 55–59.

Clark, P. K. 1973. A subordinated stochastic process model with finite variance for speculative prices. *Econometrica* 41, 135–155.

Cont, Rama, and José da Fonseca. 2002. Dynamics of implied volatility surfaces. *Quantitative Finance* 2, 45–60.

Cont, Rama, José da Fonseca, and Valdo Durrleman. 2002. Stochastic models of implied volatility surfaces. *Economic Notes* 31, 361–377.

Cox, John C., Jonathan E. Ingersoll, and Steven A. Ross. 1985. A theory of the term structure of interest rates. *Econometrica* 53, 385–407.

Demeterfi, Kresimir, Emanuel Derman, Michael Kamal, and Joseph Zou. 1999. A guide to volatility and variance swaps. *Journal of Derivatives* 6, 9–32.

Derman, Emanuel, Michael Kamal, Iraj Kani, and Joseph Z. Zou. 1996. Valuing contracts with payoffs based on realized volatility, Global Derivatives Quarterly Review, Goldman, Sachs & Co.

Derman, Emanuel, and Iraj Kani. 1994. Riding on a smile. *Risk* 7, 32–39.

————. 1998. Stochastic implied trees: Arbitrage pricing with stochastic term and strike structure of volatility. *International Journal of Theoretical and Applied Finance* 1, 61–110.

————, and Neil Chriss. 1996. Implied trinomial trees of the volatility smile. *Journal of Derivatives* 3, 7–22.

Drăgulescu, Adrian A, and Victor M Yakovenko. 2002. Probability distribution of returns in the Heston model with stochastic volatility. *Quantitative Finance* 2, 443–453.

Duffie, Darrell, Jun Pan, and Kenneth Singleton. 2000. Transform analysis and asset pricing for affine jump diffusions. *Econometrica* 68, 1343–1376.

————, and Kenneth J. Singleton. 1999. Modeling term structures of defaultable bonds. *Review of Financial Studies* 12, 687–720.

Dumas, B., J. Fleming, and R. E. Whaley. 1998. Implied volatility functions: Empirical tests. *The Journal of Finance* 53.

Dupire, Bruno. 1992. Arbitrage pricing with stochastic volatility. Proceedings of AFFI conference, Paris, reprinted in "Derivatives Pricing: The Classic Collection", edited by Peter Carr, 2004 (Risk Books, London).

———. 1994. Pricing with a smile. *Risk* 7, 18–20.

———. 1996. A unified theory of volatility, Discussion paper Paribas Capital Markets, reprinted in "Derivatives Pricing: The Classic Collection", edited by Peter Carr, 2004 (Risk Books, London).

———. 1998. A new approach for understanding the impact of volatility on option prices, ICBI Global Derivatives 98, Paris.

———. 2005. Volatility derivatives modeling, www.math.nyu.edu/carrp/mfseminar/bruno.ppt.

Durrleman, Valdo. 2005. From implied to spot volatilities. Discussion paper Department of Mathematics, Stanford University.

Finger, Christopher. 2002. Creditgrades technical document. Discussion paper Risk-Metrics Group Inc.

Finkelstein, Vladimir. 2002. Assessing default probabilities from equity markets. http://www.creditgrades.com/resources/pdf/Finkelstein.pdf.

Forde, Martin. 2006. Calibrating local-stochastic volatility models. Discussion paper Department of Mathematics, University of Bristol.

Fouque, Jean-Pierre, George Papanicolaou, and K. Ronnie Sircar. 1999. Financial modeling in a fast mean-reverting stochastic volatility environment. *Asia-Pacific Financial Markets* 6, 37–48.

———. 2000. Mean-reverting stochastic volatility. *SIAM J. Control and Optimization* 31, 470–493.

Friz, Peter, and Jim Gatheral. 2005. Valuation of volatility derivatives as an inverse problem. *Quantitative Finance* 5, 531–542.

Gastineau, Gary L., and Mark P. Kritzman. 1999. *Dictionary of Financial Risk Management* 3rd ed. New York: John Wiley & Sons, Inc.

Gatheral, Jim. 2004. A parsimonious arbitrage-free implied volatility parameterization with application to the valuation of volatility derivatives. http://www.math.nyu.edu/fellows_fin_math/gatheral/madrid2004.pdf.

Glasserman, Paul. 2004. *Monte Carlo Methods in Financial Engineering*. New York: Springer-Verlag.

Goldman, Barry, Howard Sosin, and Mary-Ann Gatto. 1979. Path dependent options: Buy at the low, sell at the high. *The Journal of Finance* 34, 1111–1127.

Hagan, Patrick S., Deep Kumar, Andrew S. Lesniewski, and Diana E. Woodward. 2002. Managing smile risk. *Wilmott Magazine*, pp. 84–108.

Heston S. 1993. A closed-form solution for options with stochastic volatility, with application to bond and currency options. *Review of Financial Studies* 6, 327–343.

———, and S. Nandi. 1998. Preference-free option pricing with path-dependent volatility: A closed-form approach. Discussion paper, Federal Reserve Bank of Atlanta.

Jeffery, Christopher. 2004. Reverse cliquets: end of the road? *Risk Magazine* 17, 20–22.

Kahl, Christian, and Peter Jäckel. 2005. Not-so-complex logarithms in the Heston model. *Wilmott Magazine*, pp. 94–103.

Kloeden, Peter E., and Eckhard Platen. 1992. *Numerical Solution of Stochastic Differential Equations: No. 23 in Applications of Mathematics.* Heidelberg: Springer-Verlag.

Lardy, Jean-Pierre. 2002. E2c: A simple model to assess default probabilities from equity markets, http://www.creditgrades.com/resources/pdf/E2C_JPM_CDconference.pdf.

Ledoit, Olivier, Pedro Santa-Clara, and Shu Yan. 2002. Relative pricing of options with stochastic volatility. Discussion paper, The Anderson School of Management, UCLA.

Lee, Roger W. 2001. Implied and local volatilities under stochastic volatility. *International Journal of Theoretical and Applied Finance* 4, 45–89.

———. 2004. The moment formula for implied volatility at extreme strikes. *Mathematical Finance* 14, 469–480.

———. 2005. Implied volatility: Statics, dynamics, and probabilistic interpretation. In R. Baeza-Yates, J. Glaz, Henryk Gzyl, Jürgen Hüsler, and José Luis Palacios, eds, *Recent Advances in Applied Probability*. Berlin: Springer Verlag.

Lewis, Alan L. 2000. *Option Valuation under Stochastic Volatility with Mathematica Code*. Newport Beach, CA: Finance Press.

Matytsin, Andrew. 1999. Modeling volatility and volatility derivatives. www.math.columbia.edu/ smirnov/Matytsin.pdf.

———. 2000. Perturbative analysis of volatility smiles. http://www.math.columbia.edu/ smirnov/matytsin2000.pdf.

Medvedev, Alexey, and Olivier Scaillet. 2004. A simple calibration procedure of stochastic volatility models with jumps by short term asymptotics. Discussion paper HEC, Genève and FAME, Université de Genève.

Merton, Robert C. 1974. On the pricing of corporate debt: The risk structure of interest rates. *The Journal of Finance* 29, 449–470.

Mikhailov, Sergei, and Ulrich Nögel. 2003. Heston's stochastic volatility model, calibration and some extensions. *Wilmott Magazine*, pp. 74–79.

Mikosch, Thomas. 1999. *Elementary Stochastic Calculus with Finance in View* Vol. 6 of *Advanced Series on Statistical Science & Applied Probability*. Singapore: World Scientific Publishing Company.

Neftci, Salih N. 2000. *An Introduction to the Mathematics of Financial Derivatives*. San Diego, CA: Academic Press.

Revuz, Daniel, and Marc Yor. 1999. *Continuous Martingales and Brownian Motion.* Berlin: Springer-Verlag.

Rubinstein, Mark. 1998. Edgeworth binomial trees. *Journal of Derivatives* 5, 20–27.

Schönbucher, Philipp. 1999. A market model of stochastic implied volatility. *Philosophical Transactions of the Royal Society, Series A* 357, 2071–2092.

Shimko, D. 1993. Bounds on probability. *Risk* 6, 33–37.

Stineman, Russell W. 1980. A consistently well-behaved method of interpolation. *Creative Computing*, pp. 54–57.

Taleb, Nassim. 1996. *Dynamic Hedging: Managing Vanilla and Exotic Options.* New York: John Wiley & Sons, Inc.

Tavella, Domingo, and Curt Randall. 2000. *Pricing Financial Instruments: The Finite Difference Method.* New York: John Wiley & Sons, Inc.

Wilmott, Paul. 2000. *Paul Wilmott on Quantitative Finance.* Chichester: John Wiley & Sons.

Index